Your Second Priority:

A Former FCC Commissioner Speaks Out

Nicholas Johnson

Lulu
Morrisville, North Carolina

May 2008

Third Edition

ISBN   978-1-4357-1836-4

TABLE OF CONTENTS

INTRODUCTION

In order to accomplish much of anything we need to prioritize. Our top priority may be making good grades in school, improving our golf score, finding a new job – or, later in life, our children. But without such a focus and measurable goal our efforts are likely to be scattered and unsuccessful.

Any activist – what Ralph Nader calls a "public citizen" – also has a top priority. It may be anything from a rather long list of possible civic undertakings, ranging from getting a corner street light installed to trying to stop a war. And like most of us, activists are not very open to abandoning their top priority for what someone else thinks their top priority *ought to be*.

As a result, when I was engaged in media reform efforts full time in the mid-1970s, as chair of the National Citizens Committee for Broadcasting, I was initially unsure how to build a media reform movement from among activists who were already hard at work on something else – namely, *their* top priority.

Because it seemed to me that media reform (like campaign finance reform) was so central to *every* public interest movement, it finally occurred to me to make the pitch, as I set forth in the last chapter of this book, that

> "Whatever is your first priority, whether it is women's rights or saving wildlife, your second priority has to be media reform. With it you at least have a chance of accomplishing your first priority. Without it, you don't have a prayer."

Many grasped the idea; it made sense to them. As a result the media reform movement grew over the years – thanks to the subsequent work of others than myself – from a few dozen individuals to its present size. For example, the media reform organization called "freepress" organizes National Conferences on Media Reform that bring thousands of activists together. http://www.freepress.net/conference/. Some attendees would identify themselves as full time media reformers, but the many with a different "top priority" are there because they understand why media reform has to be their "second priority."

As an FCC commissioner (1966-1973) I did a lot of speaking and writing. In 1970 some of that output was pulled together into a book titled, *How to Talk Back to Your Television Set*, published by Atlantic-Little Brown, and subsequently a Bantam paperback, in 1970.

After I left the commission the writing and speaking continued, although the books did not. As a result, after more than thirty-five years a rather daunting collection of material now exists that is scattered among journals, magazines and chapters in others' books, speech texts, Web uploads, and since June 2006 blog entries. Others have suggested that to make it more accessible I should consider once again pulling a small sampling of that writing into a book.

I suffer no illusion that this book will enjoy anything like the attention and interest of *Talk Back*, published during the peak of my "15 minutes of fame" as a controversial FCC commissioner. But hopefully it may be of similar use to any who do happen upon it.

It is designed to serve a similar purpose – to raise, discuss, and stimulate discussion by others of what I believe to be some of the most serious issues confronting our country and causes that should be every American's "second priority."

The material is divided into three parts. Part One, "The Basics," begins in Chapter 1 with a presentation used with individuals from other countries who want an understanding of our system ("An Autonomous Media" and "Jefferson on the Internet"). It then addresses changes in the media since the time of *Talk Back* ("What is the Press?" and "Defining the Land of the Fourth Estate" in Chapter 2). There are four pieces in Chapter 3, "Editorial Judgment and Ethics," highlighting the impact on journalism of commercial interests, political partisanship, or an excessive focus on the sensational. Part One closes with a piece about "media literacy" in Chapter 4.

Part Two, "The More Things Change . . ." leads with Chapter 5, "Forty Years of Wandering in the Wasteland," comparing "then and now" for a fortieth anniversary symposium celebrating former FCC chairman Newton Minow's speech in which he described the programming of network television as "a vast wasteland." Chapter 6, "Media Regulation and Censorship" contains a defense of the Fairness Doctrine and addresses the FCC's concerns regarding "indecency" in programming. Chapter 7 deals with the growing problem of concentration of media ownership, including the original *Atlantic* article, "The Media Barons and the Public Interest" and "Galloping Global Multi-Media Merger Mania." Although Chapter 8, "Georgia's Media Future," was prepared for legislators in the nation of Georgia, thinking about the range of options offered to them is a helpful way to explore our options as well.

Part Three, "What Lies Ahead," addresses in Chapter 9 the unprecedented challenges presented by the regulation of the Internet, existing in a "cyberspace" that is simultaneously everywhere and nowhere. Chapter 10 explores some of the new problems that digitization creates for a pre-digital copyright law ("How to Violate Copyright Without Actually Copying Anything" and "Copyright, Fair Use, and Blogging"). The book closes with Chapter 11, "Media as Politics: What's a Voter to Do," which reviews the impact of media, including the Internet, on our campaigns and governing processes.

With minor exceptions, these selections are presented in their original – and therefore often dated – form. (The original source is indicated in italics under the heading for each selection.) Hopefully, however, the reader will find them to be more than just interesting historical snapshots. For example, who owns what among American (and global) media changes over time – sometimes seemingly daily – as fewer and fewer owners come to own more and more. Today there may be more public consciousness of the dangers this poses than when the *Atlantic* published "The Media Barons and the Public Interest: An FCC Commissioner's Warning" in 1968. But the basic issues raised by the abuses from media ownership today are not that different from what they were then. The same can be said for most of the topics treated throughout this book.

Like any author, I find it impossible to credit all who have contributed to my thinking and writing in one way or another. All of us stand on the shoulders of the giants who have gone before – those whose work I have only read, such as Thomas Jefferson, and those it was my honor and pleasure to work with closely, such as U.S. Supreme Court Justice Hugo Black. As an FCC commissioner, and subsequently with the National Citizens Committee for Broadcasting, there were over 100 individuals who worked with me as personal staff or interns. Since returning to my home town of Iowa City, Iowa, and teaching at the University of Iowa's College of Law, I have benefited from the insights of my many colleagues, students, and research assistants.

Most directly involved in putting this book together, however, are five individuals. The original writing represented in this book, and such editing of the pieces as has been done, is mine. But I was not comfortable making the selections. I wanted an independent and trained eye to evaluate the thirty-five-year haystack of material, someone qualified to judge whether it contained a needle or two worth reprinting. As it happened, it was my good fortune to have a research assistant, Erin Pfaff, who was both a law student and a journalism graduate student and instructor. She was ideally trained for the task, patient and disciplined enough to be able to examine all the material, and the resulting selections are, with but few exceptions, hers.

Nor could this volume exist in its present form without the skillful touch of my assistants Lisa Schomberg, Cathy Clemens and Molly Richardson.

Finally, I would like to thank my wife, Mary Vasey, for the love and support that was apparently sufficient for her to take the time from her own writing to bring her English major-playwright editing skills to bear on some of these pieces.

So here it is, a guide to achieving "Your Second Priority," with all good wishes and hopes it may speed you on your way to achieving your first priority as well.

– Nicholas Johnson, Iowa City, Iowa, May 2008

PART ONE: The Basics

Chapter One: Media and the First Amendment

(a) An Autonomous Media

This material was originally prepared at the request of the Commission on Radio and Television Policy-Aspen Institute, as a background paper for participants from the newly independent states of the former USSR at a session held at the Aspen Wye Woods Conference Center in Maryland, May 4-7, 1994. It was designed to provide a relatively basic explanation of our First Amendment concept that the mass media are constitutionally entitled to operate free of government control. It was subsequently made available to participants at the Commission on Radio and Television Policy: Central and East Europe Public Broadcasting and Globalization Conference, Vienna, Austria, September 19 and 20, 1997, and those attending the Journalist in Cyberspace: A Warsaw Journalism Center International Conference, Warsaw, Poland, October 11-12, 1997.

The First Amendment: An American Case Study

Each nation's broadcasting system is a function of its history, economic and political systems. There are similarities among the systems that emphasize state control; similarities among those that utilize public corporations; and similarities among capitalist, advertiser-supported broadcasting systems. But each country's system is also unique in a variety of ways – and probably should be.[1]

This chapter emphasizes the American system of broadcasting. That emphasis has been chosen not because it is the only system, or the best, but because it is (1) one of the major systems, (2) is seen as a model, or benchmark, by many (whether rightly or wrongly), (3) demonstrates a mix of government, public, and private systems, (4) well illustrates the complexity, strengths and weaknesses of one country's approach, and (5) is best known to the author.

In order to understand the "autonomy" of U.S. media,[2] it is useful to begin with the First Amendment of the United States Constitution, and the reasons why Americans think it is important.

The relevant language of the First Amendment is very general. It says, simply, "Congress[3] shall make no law abridging the freedom of speech or of the press."[4]

The real meaning and effect of this language can only be understood once one has at least a general understanding of our systems of government, and especially the American court system.

Where the First Amendment fits in the U.S. governmental and legal system.

The U.S. has fifty-one legal systems, each with its own executives, legislatures, and courts. One is the national, or what we call "federal," system (because it includes a "federation" of states). This includes the President, Congress (a "House" and "Senate"), and federal judiciary, or courts.[5] The other fifty systems are those of the fifty states that make up "the United States of America."[6]

Although the First Amendment seems to be a restraint limited to "Congress," as interpreted by the courts all governmental units (from the President to mayors of cities) are subject to the restraints of the U.S. Constitution (as interpreted by the judges).

The judges who preside over the federal courts are supposed to be – and in almost every sense, truly and totally *are* – independent of any influence from the President or Congress. They are selected by the President, and approved by the Senate. But once approved they are judges until they die (or resign), cannot be removed or intimidated, nor may their salaries be reduced. Most presidents, legislators and judges have taken this "judicial independence" very seriously and honor it in both letter and spirit.[7]

It is important to understand this genuine independence of the judges in order to understand the true meaning, and operation, of the First Amendment of the Constitution.

What would happen if the constitutional protection from government interference in the operations of newspapers and broadcasting stations was only enforced by judges who could be punished, or removed, by the President at any time? Such a constitutional "guarantee" would not provide much protection for the newspaper editor, or broadcaster, who wished to criticize the President.

Where the First Amendment fits in the hearts of the people.

Any law, to be effective, must be understood and accepted in the hearts of a majority of the people. The First Amendment is no exception. It is not enough that it is "the law." Officials and citizens alike must understand *why* it is a good idea to permit the expression of information and ideas with which they disagree. The information and opinions may in fact be ones that they hate, that may make them look very foolish (or corrupt), and that may make them very angry.[8] Clearly, there are disadvantages to free speech; it's just that those disadvantages are believed by most Americans to be more than outweighed by the advantages.

The idea of "free speech and press" is not a new one in the U.S. The country has lived with it for over 200 years. It is an idea Americans grow up with. They experience it, learn about it in schools, and hear it debated on radio and television.[9] Even secondary school and college students, who publish school newspapers, argue with professors and college presidents (who may wish to censor something students want in the paper) that the students "have First Amendment rights."[10]

There are individuals (or groups, or officials) who are angered by particular ideas and propose that speaking those ideas should be illegal. Sometimes they convince a significant number of citizens that "something should be done" about the expression of ideas that they don't like.[11]

But there are also citizens' organizations – such as the "American Civil Liberties Union" and "People for the American Way" – that stand up for the First Amendment, and almost always convince a majority of Americans that "free speech," even awful speech, is better than censorship. They will sometimes quote a former U.S. Supreme Court Justice, Louis Brandeis, who advised by way of a concurring opinion in *Whitney v. California*, 274 U.S. 357, 377 (1927), "If there be time to expose through discussion the falsehood and fallacies, to avert the evil by the processes of education, the remedy to be applied is more speech, not enforced silence." And the independent judges have been very careful to protect First Amendment rights.

What are the values and consequences of the First Amendment?

So, why are people willing to tolerate the expression of information and opinion they dislike? Why do we have a First Amendment? Why is the country better off with it than without it? Or, if not better off, in what ways is life different because of it? What are the values and consequences of the First Amendment?

As the reader has probably guessed, a great deal has been written about these questions over the last 200 years or so – by judges, professors, journalists, lawyers, political scientists, and many others. Everyone, it seems, has an opinion about the matter. So it is not possible to summarize all of that literature here. But even a brief survey can be useful.

Arguments affirming the value of the First Amendment fall essentially into five categories: (1) its role in meeting the necessity of an informed citizenry in an effective system of self-government, (2) its importance to the "marketplace of ideas" from which truth is more likely to emerge, (3) its relationship to the "checking value" of the media, as it watches for, and reports, abuses by government and other large institutions, (4) its bearing on individuals' "self-actualization," growth, basic liberty, and personal freedom, and (5) the "safety valve" it provides, permitting dissidents the opportunity to express their dissatisfaction verbally, rather than through violence.

Following is a brief explanation of each:

(1) Self-governing citizenry. In theory – and also in practice – "democracy" means that each citizen is a "government official" of sorts, with a responsibility for first becoming informed about the issues of the day, then forming and expressing opinions about what should be done, and finally trying to persuade others to agree with her or his ideas. Ultimately from this process of becoming informed, and trying to persuade, emerges a popular consensus as to what action should result. For example, for decades there has been a very active public debate about how we should provide health care to all of our citizens. (We do not yet have a consensus on that one.)

Most Americans recognize their citizenship responsibility, think self-governing is a precious thing – even something worth fighting to protect – and make some effort to participate.[12]

Those who wrote the U.S. Constitution believed that if the opportunity of self-governing was to be meaningful, it was absolutely essential that citizens have the freedom to get access to as much information and opinion as possible[13] – and to contribute personally to the public dialogue. Any governmental effort to restrict that flow of information and opinion would be a death blow to the whole idea of self-governance, something "un-American," undemocratic, and unconstitutional.[14]

(2) Marketplace of ideas. What is "truth"? Clearly, its meaning depends on the context in which it is found. A religious truth may come from an ancient text, or a religious leader. A scientific truth may come only from the results of experiments that can be replicated by other scientists. A political truth may be little more than the opinion of the majority at the moment.

But however one defines "truth," the search will certainly be aided by the widest possible access to the full range of available information and opinion.

This is sometimes referred to as having access to a "marketplace of ideas." All possible information, ideas, theories and opinions are laid out on tables in the market. The ideas that "sell" come to be viewed as "truth" in that "marketplace."[15]

So this is yet another reason for, or consequence of, free speech. Regardless of the form of government, it is believed that a society will gain in every way – in prosperity, culture, science, the arts, and politics – to the extent that its citizens' search for truth is free and open.

(3) Checking value. Free speech and press are sometimes called "a fourth branch of government."[16] To speak of print and broadcast journalists in this way simply presumes, without even discussing the matter, that they are autonomous of government.[17] This value of the First Amendment does not relate to the *content* of speech, as such, but rather to the *process* and consequences of gathering and disseminating information.

The need for a "checking value" is based on the assumption that every institution in society, not just government, is capable of becoming ingrown, resistant to change, secretive, fundamentally corrupt, and more interested in perpetuating itself than in doing what it was created to do.[18] This can be true whether the institutions are businesses, universities, churches, hospitals, or military and police units.[19]

Of all the ways to avoid these tendencies and provide a "check" on such abuses, one of the most effective is believed to be free and independent journalism. Reporters can go anywhere, ask anything, demand documents, take pictures, listen to complainants, and be quite innovative in uncovering abuses.[20] This is called "investigative reporting." Because the reading, listening and viewing audience likes to learn about such abuses or scandals, those who own the media are willing to have them reported and advertisers are willing to advertise in such media.[21] Thus, another value of the First Amendment is that it helps to keep other institutions in the society somewhat more honest and efficient.

(4) Self-actualization. Another argument for the First Amendment is also independent of the content of speech. It is a value related to concepts like "liberty," "freedom," "self-esteem," "self-expression," "personal growth and development," "education" and "culture." For these, some use the single expression "self-actualization." By this is meant the process by which an individual realizes, through his or her effort, as much of their potential as possible.[22] Such a process necessarily includes the opportunity to become informed, educated, cultured – and to express oneself intellectually, creatively, and artistically.

For a government, or other institution, to stifle free thought and expression, or to forbid some subjects or opinions to be expressed, obviously impedes individuals' self-actualization. For the purposes of this category, the ideas expressed may contribute nothing whatsoever to the society's self-governing, search for truth, or checking value. If they contribute to the growth of the individual in question, this value of the First Amendment is being served.

(5) Safety valve. A safety valve on a boiler can release steam before the boiler builds up pressure and explodes. The First Amendment also serves this purpose for a society.[23] A famous civil rights leader in America, Dr. Martin Luther King, once said, "Having been denied access to radio and television we have had to write our most persuasive essays with the blunt pen of marching ranks." Fortunately, he was an exponent of "non-violent" strategies for change. But his reference to a "march" as an "essay" helps make the point. Other, less skilled "essayists," have chosen to shoot, loot and burn in order to be heard.[24]

So this final value furthered by the First Amendment is also unrelated to the precise content of the speech. It is, perhaps, related more to the preceding value of self-actualization. Here the value is the belief that, if people are free to present their grievances through speech and writing, if they have the opportunity to get the attention of their fellow citizens and officials, if they have the feeling that they have been "heard," they are much less likely to use violence as their preferred method of protest and reform.[25]

Free Speech in Practice

Who's abridging the speech?

As mentioned above, although the First Amendment speaks only of "Congress" being prohibited from making laws abridging the freedom of speech or of the press the word "Congress" has been expanded by the courts to include all units of government.[26] So what about "abridgments" of speech by institutions and individuals other than governmental units? With few exceptions, unnecessary to our discussion, citizens enjoy no protection whatsoever.

Most newspapers and magazines have something like a "letters to the editor" column. Anyone can send a letter for publication, which may be, in effect, a short opinion article. What if the newspaper publisher disagrees with the opinion expressed or fears that it will anger readers (or advertisers)? What if he or she is prejudiced against the author for some reason? Must the letter be published?

The answer is that the publisher has no obligation to print the letter. The First Amendment only applies to units of government. The publisher is not a unit of government. Therefore, the publisher is in no way restrained by the First Amendment.

Nor do reporters and writers have free speech rights. They are employees. It is the owner of the newspaper, the publisher, who has the First Amendment's protection. The publisher, and the editors whom she or he hires (and can fire), can re-write the reporter's article, "censor" it entirely, and – ultimately, if they want to – fire the reporter. The only way reporters can acquire full First Amendment rights is to purchase their own newspapers or broadcast stations.

Even if a newspaper attacks someone it has no obligation to give that person an opportunity to buy space in the paper to reply. The Supreme Court held a state law unconstitutional that was an effort to provide such a right. The Court said such a law would violate the newspaper's First Amendment rights to censor from its pages anything it chose.[27]

Not even broadcasting is treated differently – in spite of the scarcity of broadcast frequencies. There are some exceptions.[28] But in general, even though a broadcaster has commercial time for sale he or she can refuse to sell to someone if the broadcaster does not like the message.[29]

The values underlying the First Amendment, discussed above,[30] are of course equally applicable regardless of who is doing the abridging of free speech. If a corporate owner directly, or in response to advertiser pressure, keeps particular information or opinion from being printed or broadcast, the audience is just as ignorant as if the censoring was done by some unit of government. And yet the First Amendment provides no "autonomy" for journalists, or members of the public, from *corporate* censorship.

Matters of Grace and Matters of Right.

In understanding free speech in practice, it is important to distinguish two very different circumstances.

One is free speech as a matter of legal right, based in the First Amendment of the Constitution and enforceable in courts of law.

The other is free speech as a matter of grace. By "grace" we mean an opportunity to speak publicly that has been granted a speaker or writer by a broadcaster or publisher because the owner wants to do so.

For example, a city could not refuse to grant an organization the right to use an auditorium owned by the city, and available for rent to public groups, because the mayor did not like what the organization's speaker was going to say. It could not refuse to grant the organization a permit to have a demonstration, or parade, because of content. For it to do so would be a violation of the First Amendment. The organization could go to court and force the city to make the auditorium, or streets, available.

In fact, most publishers and broadcasters, as a matter of grace, permit quite a variety of viewpoints through the media they own. They may deliberately seek out "liberal" and "conservative" spokespersons. Some will publicize letters from the audience that are very critical of a station's programming or newspaper's stories and editorials. They may invite guests onto their programs, or editorial pages, whose views represent a wide range of ideologies different from those of the owner.

It is important to understand this point.

It is not the case that owners always censor their employees' and others' speech to reflect the owner's views. They may have any one of a number of other motives in mind. (1) More openness makes it easier to hire, and keep, good journalists. (2) More diversity and controversy may increase the number of readers, or television watchers. Since publishers and station owners are in the business of selling their audience to advertisers, the larger the audience the richer the owner becomes. (3) A third reason may be the owner's genuine commitment to the values of the First Amendment, even though not required by law. Whatever the reasons may be in each case, the fact is that a tremendous range of information and opinion is available to the American audience from thousands of radio and television stations, newspapers and magazines.[31]

The point is simply that the owner always retains the *potential power* to keep from the public any information or opinion he or she chooses to censor. Such variety as the owner provides, or permits, comes as "a matter of grace" not as "a matter of right."

Autonomy and Democracy

A democratic society confronts a genuine dilemma with regard to its mass media.

The First Amendment is designed to produce the fertile soil in which self-government can grow, make possible the search for "truth" in a marketplace of ideas, the pursuit of self-actualization, a check on institutional abuses, and a safety valve alternative to violent strategies for change.[32]

If these values are to be realized, units of government cannot be given the power to determine what is "acceptable" speech. Speech must be "autonomous" of such governmental control.

But does this mean that there is no role for democratic participation in the content of speech? For many years there has been a debate in America about the impact of "violence" in the media on the real (and increasing) levels of violence in our communities. If a majority of the American people want some control over the television programming that they and their children watch, should they be permitted to have it? Because of genuine commitment to First Amendment principles, even those public officials advocating such controls have been very hesitant to propose governmental action. (They often speak of industry "self-regulation" – which, historically, has not worked.)

Can we make a meaningful distinction between (1) restraints on speech that reflect democratically determined standards of propriety and social values, on the one hand, and, on the other, (2) restraints imposed by a political party, or government, that seeks to control the media to cover up its mistakes, oppress its opposition, and stay in power? Do we have to forbid any of the former in order to guarantee there will be none of the latter? Do citizens have no right to help shape the standards of these privately-owned media institutions that, some believe, have more influence on a culture (especially on its children) than family, church and school combined? This is an ongoing debate, and one that contributes substantially to the complexities in the choices between "state controlled" and "autonomous" media.

Why do these problems, this dilemma, arise? The desire for, and need for, some measure of governmental "regulation" comes about precisely because of the insistence of large corporate media firms that they have the power to censor. In spite of their near-monopoly power, the courts have acquiesced in the notion that the constitutional right to speak necessarily includes the right to keep others from speaking. That being the case, some form of regulation is demanded by the public. Is there an alternative to some form of regulation?[33] Yes.

The concept of "public access."

"Access" to media can be used to describe a variety of opportunities, or rights.

It could refer to a right to receive information and ideas. That might take the form of importing literature from a country from which one's government has forbidden importation. It may be a desire to have a shortwave radio receiver, or "satellite dish," capable of receiving radio or television signals from other countries when such receivers are prohibited.

"Access" is also used to describe an individual's right to enter information into the near-monopoly conduits that constitute our mass media: a city's only (or dominant) newspaper, radio or television station. To distinguish this meaning from the right to receive, it will be referred to as a "right of entry."

As discussed above,[34] there is no such legally enforceable "right of entry" at this time into near-monopoly newspapers and broadcasting facilities.[35] The only exception would be the so-called "community access" channels on local cable television systems.[36]

Thus, the point for now is simply that such an approach would be an alternative to government regulation of near-monopolies. If it is true that "the answer to speech is more speech"[37] then a "right of entry" can substitute for virtually all alternative regulation. Citizens need not rely on a "fairness doctrine."[38] They, personally, could get entry into the main conduits of media distribution to say whatever they wanted, however they wanted. They would have a personal remedy.

Such a system would be, in many ways, the purest form of "autonomy." But it would require a radical modification of media industry practice – not to mention Supreme Court constitutional law decisions!

Even if such forms of direct access were available, would journalists, politicians and the general public make use of it?

Self-censorship.

"Censorship" is normally thought of as something imposed from the outside, usually from some branch of government. But one of the most invidious forms of censorship is self-imposed. It is also probably the most common.

Journalists may engage in self-censorship, avoiding the story they know will displease their publisher, editor, colleagues – or other powerful individuals who may be able to do them harm.[39] Self-censorship may come from lack of courage, a desire to avoid controversy, or perhaps even an unwillingness to risk getting fired. It may come from the social pressure of neighbors, or co-workers. It is re-enforced by laziness: it takes a lot more time and trouble to investigate a story than to re-write a news release.[40] It may be very difficult to get the editorial approval to take on such an assignment – or the budget and other resources necessary to carry it out successfully.

Whatever the reasons, the impact on audience knowledge (and ignorance) is fully as great as if a government censor were sitting in the newsroom.

And similar, self-imposed pressures apply to everyone, journalist or not. Those who are not experienced, or lack self confidence, in speaking out in public may remain quiet and shy. Few will want to risk the anger of powerful individuals in the community. Many individuals want to avoid association with controversy rather than seeking it out.

So even though "access" is theoretically available to all, it may not be exercised in fact.[41]

Conclusion

The purpose of this chapter is to provide a shared base of information and insight (however flawed!) into some of the issues surrounding "autonomy of the media". It attempts to show both the virtues and values of a free and independent media, and the difficulties in creating such a condition in any country – including the United States.

Appendix: Alternative Systems of Broadcasting

This chapter has been premised on the assumption that the only choices for national media (television) systems are "state controlled" and "advertiser-supported, for profit, 'autonomous' (from state control) media corporations." That is, of course a false assumption. There are many other alternatives.

(a) In the first place, although broadcasting often is centrally controlled it need not be. Radio began in the United States as local stations. Networks only came later. In fact, it is only local stations that are licensed; networks as such are not. The elected officials who created the first laws (Radio Act of 1927) were very concerned about central control over such a powerful medium. Much of the law and FCC regulation is designed to encourage the distribution of this power throughout the country. (Local owner-operators are preferred as licensees; there are limits on transmitting power, the number of stations one licensee can operate, the terms of network contracts with local stations; and there is a responsibility to serve the needs of the local community.) By contrast, the Japanese public broadcasting system, NHK, primarily produces its programs centrally and "local stations" do little more than transmit them to television receivers throughout the cities and mountainous country.

(b) A distinction must be drawn between "government" broadcasting and "public" broadcasting. The U.S. has both. Government broadcasting is illustrated by the Voice of America, Radio Marti (broadcasting to Cuba), Radio Free Europe, Radio Liberty, and the Armed Forces Radio Service. (These services are forbidden, by law, to broadcast within the USA.) The content of their broadcasts represents the position of the USA government.

"Public" broadcasting, by contrast, may be funded in whole or in part by the government, but is organized so as to be (for most purposes) independent of any political or governmental influence on content. Examples from other countries would include NHK (Japan), BBC (Great Britain), Sverges Radio (Sweden), ARD and ZDF (Germany). In the U.S., public broadcasting includes the Corporation for Public Broadcasting, Public Broadcasting Service, and National Public Radio. Unlike government broadcasting, public broadcasting may end up being very independent indeed from the government and political party in power. It may even contribute to the defeat of those in power. To make this point I have sometimes observed that "the BBC is more independent of the British government than NBC is independent of the U.S. government."

(c) Commercial, or advertiser-supported, broadcasting is the dominant form of organization in the U.S. There are commercial networks (ABC, CBS, NBC and Fox, among others), and local "affiliates" of these networks. They are a business. Note, however, that the business they are in is not the business of programming. It is the business of selling the audience (the product), to the advertiser (the consumer) – at a cost per 1000 viewers. This means that the programming is merely designed to attract the largest possible crowd. Violence is a useful, and economically successful, way to do that.

(d) Although never an economic success, "subscription television" is possible and has been tried in the U.S. This involves "scrambling" the television broadcast signal from a station, and then selling a subscriber a "descrambler" box to see the programming (often new movies).

Cable television systems offer channels called "pay cable." These have been economically successful. As the name suggests, they are program services for which the subscriber must pay an additional monthly fee (usually about $10 per channel). Examples would be HBO ("Home Box Office"), "The Disney Channel," or "Showtime."

Subscription television and pay cable are examples of a broadcasting business that does involve programming. Money is made by selling programming to the viewer, not by selling the viewer to an advertiser. (Normally there would be no advertising on a pay service.)

(e) Educational broadcasters. The licenses for "public" radio or television stations need to be held by some organization or individual. The licensee may be a state.

(WOI-TV, an ABC affiliate, was for many years owned by the State of Iowa's Board of Regents (the committee regulating the state's higher education).) It may be a city. (The City of New York owns station WNYC-TV/FM.) It may be a group of citizens. (WETA-TV in Washington, D.C. gets its call letters from the "Educational Television Association" of Washington.) But, most often, it is an educational institution (usually a university). (WAMU-FM in Washington is owned by American University. WSUI-AM in Iowa City was given those call letters because it is owned by what used to be called the State University of Iowa.)

(f) Other organizations. Churches may own stations. The Mormon Church owns KSL-TV/AM in Salt Lake City, Utah (among many others). The Chicago Federation of Labor gave its name to WCFL in Chicago.

(g) "Community" stations. Citizens may organize, and contribute money, to support stations (in addition to "public" stations). Foundations may help with financial support. An example would be the Pacifica station group, including WBAI-FM in New York City, and KPFK-FM in Los Angeles. These are usually among the freest of all stations in their willingness to present unpopular points of view. (One may surmise that this has something to do with the lack of dependence on corporate funding. For commercial stations such dependence takes the form of corporate advertising. For public stations it takes the form of corporate "underwriting" (recently coming to be closer and closer to the same thing as advertising).)

The point of this extended description of alternatives is simply that, to the extent one wishes to encourage "autonomy," there may well be choices preferable to either pure "state control" or pure "commercial corporate" broadcasting.

Appendix: "Autonomy" is not "Independence"

Merely because broadcasters are not employees of the government does not mean that they are in every way independent of the government. For many reasons, commercial broadcasters may provide support for "the establishment" (the wealthy, or those managing large institutions of all kinds) in general, and the government in particular.

(a) In the first place, the owners of major media in the U.S. are at least millionaires, if not billionaires. They are part of the establishment. They are no more comfortable seeming to criticize their friends and golfing buddies than a labor union president would be criticizing unproductive union rules, or a professor writing about unethical university practices. They like to be well thought of by government officials – just as government officials like to socialize with millionaires and business leaders.

(b) An organization called FAIR publishes a magazine of media criticism called *Extra!* It has run a number of articles analyzing the tendency of news and interview programs to tend to limit the choice of guests to middle-of-the-road establishment figures. It says the guests tend to range from "center" to "right," and are rarely from organizations outside the government or corporate sphere, such as schools, churches, or "public interest" organizations. These choices may well be unconscious; producers invite as guests people they know. But the consequence is a media tendency to support government positions on issues. (It should be noted that another organization, Accuracy in Media (AIM), takes the contrary view: that the media have a liberal-left bias.)

(c) Media owners may fear retribution by federal government agencies with regulatory authority over them, and enormous discretion. The Post Office determines who gets reductions in postal rates for publications. The FCC gives (and can take away) broadcasters' licenses. (Its statutory standard for review is the vague "public interest.") The Federal Trade Commission (FTC) regulates advertising content in publications and broadcasts.

(d) When broadcasting stations are owned by large corporations with other subsidiaries ("conglomerates") they may be tempted to use their media power to serve other corporate interests. They may be a multi-billion-dollar provider of goods and services to the Defense Department (like GE, which owns NBC). They may have interests in tariff and trade policy (like the motion picture studios during the recent GATT negotiations). Agencies that enforce the antitrust laws (those prohibiting monopolies and anti-competitive business practices), such as the Department of Justice and FTC, have great discretion as to when they will act. A company may benefit from subsidy programs (such as those for agriculture, shipping, or mineral rights on public land). Hundreds of other examples could be provided. When billions of dollars are at stake, and politicians are notoriously overly concerned about their media "image," the temptation for media firms to curry favor with the government is large.

(e) Government officials may attack the media in speeches (called "jawboning"). President Nixon used this technique – often having his Vice President, Spiro Agnew, make the speeches. But all presidents have done it to some extent. President Johnson used to call network presidents directly to complain about their coverage of the Viet Nam war. President Clinton lashed out at the media in an interview for the magazine *Rolling Stone*. Media executives do not like to be the center of controversy, especially when they are being attacked. Members of the House and Senate can hold hearings. For example, Senator Simon once put public pressure on the networks to reduce violence in programming. Many other examples could be provided. The point is simply that there are many ways in which a government can exert influence over the media besides treating it as an agency of that government.

Endnotes

1. It turns out that although the choices and differences between "autonomous" and "state controlled" media may at first seem simple, the more one explores the issues

the more complex they become. This may be basic material, but for that very reason it is useful for Americans to review and understand it before proceeding.

2. Although the CRTP-Aspen group emphasizes "television," this chapter refers to "media." The word "media" is meant to include newspapers, magazines, radio, television, cable, and other forms of expression. "Other," today, would include such things as video tapes, video games, and CD-ROM "multi-media" disks often including related text, pictures, animation, video, music, speech, and so forth, such as the Microsoft "Encarta" CD-ROM encyclopedia. Some of these are sometimes described as "inter-active" media (because they require, or permit, the user to do something more than merely "watch television"). "Virtual reality" seems to be next in line for our attention – and money. The reason for using the entire category, rather than "television" alone, is because (a) each is important, (b) the issues are similar for all, (c) each involves a form of "free speech," and (d) the corporate structures, regulation, software, hardware and telecommunications networks are now so interconnected that it is hard to know, for example, where "computers" stop and "television" begins.

3. The courts have interpreted "Congress" to mean any and all governmental units: federal, state, and city.

4. It also provides for freedom of religion, freedom to gather in groups ("assembly"), and freedom to send letters of complaint, or requests, to government officials ("petition"). The phrase "or of the press" has provoked a debate, among Supreme Court judges and others, regarding whether the corporate, commercial media are constitutionally intended to have more First Amendment rights than any ordinary American citizen. We need not explore that here.

5. There are federal "district courts" for trials, "courts of appeals" for review, and the "Supreme Court" for final review.

6. Each state also has its executive (a "Governor"), legislature, and court system. The states are not totally "autonomous" from the federal government, but most Americans would think them mostly autonomous (for example, they have separate taxing systems, roads, schools, police and military units). They are not administrative units of the federal government. These fifty-one systems are sometimes characterized as but two: a federal system and a state system. It is not necessary for our purposes to provide details about the ways in which these two governmental systems (federal and state) cooperate – and conflict – with each other.

7. State court judges may also be appointed for life, but some must be elected, or re-elected, from time to time. They may be less independent, therefore, than federal judges. Most think of themselves as independent and not subject to the direct control of a governor or state legislature. However, they are, of course, required to follow the interpretations of the U.S. Constitution announced by the federal Supreme Court.

8. An example in the spring of 1994 was the "Whitewater" controversy involving the President and Mrs. Clinton. (The details are not clear as of March 1994, but appear to involve perfectly legal financial transactions of little value or consequence occurring many years ago.) Many Americans believe the Whitewater story has received far too much attention by the media, to the point of seriously interfering with the process of governing the nation. The author is among the critics: "Bill Clinton is not sleeping on the job but are you?" The *Cedar Rapids Gazette*, Jan. 30, 1994, p. 6A ("Deliberately crippling a president makes even less sense than crippling an Olympic skater"). However, because of the First Amendment, President Clinton is powerless to curtail this "investigative journalism." And most Americans – including probably President Clinton himself – would agree that he should be powerless to control it. President Thomas Jefferson, who suffered his own share of questionable attacks from the press, once wrote, "The basis of our government being the opinion of the people, the very first object should be to keep that right; and were it left to me to decide whether we should have a government without newspapers, or newspapers without a government, I should not hesitate a moment to prefer the latter." Thomas Jefferson, Letter to Colonel Edward Carrington, January 16, 1787, in Boyd, Jullian P., ed., Papers of Thomas Jefferson, v. 11, p. 49 (1955).

9. In 1994 a poll was taken of Americans' attitudes about the First Amendment. Of those polled, 65 percent opposed restrictions on newspapers and television stations; 29 percent supported restrictions. But majorities also believed government restrictions were valid under some circumstances: to guard military secrets (69 percent), to discourage terrorism (60 percent), to restrict explicit sex (59 percent), and to discourage "unnecessary violence" (52 percent). David Morris (Associated Press), reprinted, "Americans support free press – to a point," The Daily Iowan, March 16, 1994, p. A1.

10. The fact that those who assert First Amendment rights may be wrong in their interpretation of the law is another matter. Many are. The point is simply that many people know *something* about their free speech rights and believe they protect them when they express unpopular opinions.

11. (a) Even shortly after the First Amendment was enacted, Congress passed a "sedition" law prohibiting criticism of government. (b) The U.S. has occasionally contained a substantial number of citizens who believed that talking about Marxist, or other communist, ideas was "un-American" and should be punished in some way (most recently with U.S. Senator, Joseph McCarthy, in the 1950s). (c) In more recent times the government prohibited some federally-funded health professionals to talk about the possibility of abortion with pregnant women.

The point is simply that generally, and at least in these examples, proponents of free speech usually win out, often very promptly, and the restrictions are removed. For attitudes of Americans about the First Amendment see the poll results in endnote 9, above. As only one illustration (randomly chosen from potentially hundreds) that censorship is an ongoing subject of attention and vigorous debate, one day's *New*

York Times contained three letters in the "letters to the editor" section on the topic. They involved the play "Peter Pan," the writings of Annie Dillard and Alice Walker, Harriet Beecher Stowe's book Uncle Tom's Cabin, Meredith Tax's children's book Families, and the movie "Schindler's List." "School Censors Violate the Rights of Children," *New York Times*, March 18, 1994, p. A10.

12. Of course, there will always be those who, for whatever reason, do not. In the same way, there are always some students, parents, doctors, or other professionals, who don't take their responsibilities very seriously either. Some citizens don't even bother to vote. But a democracy cannot force people to govern themselves. It can only give them that opportunity. Although the author is often critical of the failures of the U.S. political and mass media systems, he also wishes to acknowledge the extent to which they are not only working, but vigorously doing so. At almost any hour of the day or night there are numerous, ongoing opportunities for citizens to express their views on radio, television and cable "talk shows" of various kinds – not to mention the many guest interview programs (onto which one must be invited, but which together present a range of views). Some are broadcast nationally and available to all citizens, others are only broadcast locally. In addition to broadcasting outlets there are also, of course, the numerous newspaper and magazine "op-ed" and "letters" pages, and increasing numbers of "electronic bulletin boards" and other computer communications opportunities. Home computers also make "online" or "desktop publishing" opportunities available to millions. And much of the dialogue goes on over family dinner tables, in coffee shops, and around the water coolers at work. The discussion feeds back upon itself, public opinion is formed, and then shifts. There is a constant polling of this public opinion by numerous media, political and commercial firms. Political and public interest organizations propose actions based on public opinion – everything from putting in a new street light locally to banning cigarette smoking in public buildings, or going to war. Government officials often change policies based on their perception of public opinion – without even waiting for a formal public protest. In short, the self-governing process really does work in practice in its own imprecise and imperfect way. It is more than just a theoretical model.

13. Although not the subject of this paper, the provision of free public education, free public libraries, and reduced postal rates for newspapers, magazines, books, and library materials were also early expressions of official commitment to the informational needs of a self-governing society. More modern forms of this recognition are the creation of "National Public Radio" and public television in the 1960s, and the Clinton Administration's efforts to make government documents available to citizens electronically, online, by way of Internet connections to government computers.

14. In practice, the values of the First Amendment are often balanced against other interests of the society (such as protecting children from obscenity, requiring contents labels on food and pharmaceutical products, or maintaining secrecy in wartime about, say, the movement of troops). But at least one Supreme Court judge

has pointed out that the literal language of the First Amendment (unlike, say, the Fourth Amendment, which protects citizens from "unreasonable searches" of their homes by government officials), does not merely prohibit *unreasonable* restraints on free speech. It provides that "Congress shall make *no law*" abridging free speech. Another Supreme Court judge referred to the "preferred position" of the First Amendment when weighing values. Whatever language or analyses they use, virtually all judges recognize that there is something very special and precious about free speech.

15. I have sometimes noted the distinction between "a marketplace of ideas" and "the ideas of the marketplace." (a) One thing meant by that refers to the influence of advertisers on the content of advertiser-supported newspapers and broadcasting. For example, lung cancer (from smoking cigarettes) is a greater health risk for American women than breast cancer. Health, nutrition and exercise are big topics for "women's magazines." And yet, those women's magazines that accept cigarette advertising write very little about these 450,000 deaths a year. (b) That such outlets are owned by large corporations, possibly engaged in other, controversial, businesses about which their journalists need to report, may also affect which information and thoughts are permitted to become "ideas of the marketplace." For example, one of the three or four major television networks, NBC, is owned by one of the country's largest corporations: General Electric. At the time it purchased NBC some wondered if GE, which is in the nuclear power station business, might use NBC News to help promote public acceptance, and public utility purchase of, nuclear power stations. At about that time NBC broadcast a pro-nuclear power documentary regarding nuclear power plants in France.

16. The first three branches of government would be, as discussed above (see text and endnote at note call 6), the legislative, executive and judicial. The federal "independent regulatory commissions" ("independent" of what, and why, and to what extent we need not pursue here) have also been referred to as a fourth branch of government. The Federal Communications Commission would be an example of such an agency. The author is aware that the Russian expression, "fourth branch of government," had an entirely different meaning during the Soviet era. In political rhetoric in the U.S. the phrase has no negative, or cynical, overtones.

17. Autonomous, yes, but see "Appendix: 'Autonomy' is not 'Independence,'" below, for some significant restraints on the exercise of real independence.

18. The use of the word "check," or "checking value," helps explain why the media would be described as a "fourth branch of government." See endnote 16. The three branches of government are said to be a "check" on each other. For example, the President appoints officials, but the Senate must approve them. The President requests money, but the House appropriates it. The Congress passes laws, but the courts can render them void, as unconstitutional. The ways in which the media function as an analogous check are explained in the text.

19. A society, of course, has many other potential ways to investigate such institutions and hold them to account. The legal system is of some use. There may be regulatory agencies for monopolies. Legislative committees can hold hearings. Various police agencies, with a variety of techniques, may play a role. The institution may have internal procedures to watch for, and try to avoid, criminal violations or other abuses.

20. (a) Many of these opportunities are legally enforceable rights of reporters. Although outside the scope of this paper, a couple of examples would include "public trials," "sunshine" or "open meetings" laws, and the "Freedom of Information Act" (providing that, with some exceptions, reporters and citizens alike can get access to most paper in government files). President Clinton's Administration has recently opened up millions of formerly-classified documents in what *The New York Times* has called "the least secretive policy on Government records since the birth of the modern national security apparatus in 1947." Tim Weiner, "U.S. Plans Secrecy Overhaul To Open Millions of Records," *New York Times*, March 18, 1994, p. A1. (b) Of course, reporters may have some assistance. But that only makes their "checking value" function more obvious and effective. "Whistle-blower" refers to someone within an institution who refuses to maintain secrecy about an abuse (that is, they "blow the whistle" to attract attention). Whistle-blowers sometimes provide information, often in confidence, to reporters. This might take the form of machine copies of documents mailed to a reporter in a plain envelope with no return address. (c) This option – "going to the media," as it is called – may be thought of as analogous to someone turning to the courts, or an elected legislator, for relief.

21. But see endnote 15 for examples of results of "investigative reporting" not desired by owners or advertisers, and see "Appendix: 'Autonomy' is not 'Independence,'" for illustrations of government influence on the content of the "autonomous" media.

22. Even the U.S. Army has used this concept in its efforts to recruit new soldiers with its motto (in a singing television commercial): "Be all that you can be, in the Army."

23. The "safety valve" value may be thought of as (a) a cynical, meaningless grant from those who control the society to those who do not, in an effort to reduce any effective (that is, violent) efforts at change by the latter that would reduce the wealth or power of the former. Or it may be thought of as (b) a very real commitment to democratic rule, including the possibility of loss of power, based on a belief that it is wrong to silence any group in the society – whether or not they would be likely to turn violent if suppressed. For our purposes we need not take sides in that debate.

24. Following the arson, looting, and rioting in downtown Los Angeles in 1965, one of the young rioters was quoted as saying, "What we do last night, maybe it wasn't right. But ain't nobody come down here and listen to us before" – again making the

link between speech and violence. As Dr. King put it, "A riot is the language of the unheard." Many instances of airline hijacking, or hostage taking, turn out to involve both a speech-related frustration on the part of those committing the crime, and a desire (sometimes demand) for access to the media to tell their story.

25. Whether this reason is valid is another matter. Some argue that by permitting the expression of grievances one only raises the expectations of those doing the complaining, increases the anger of those already upset, contributes to the organization of what may turn out to be even larger groups of individuals willing to engage in violence, and thereby intensifies the danger of disintegrating the society. Nonetheless, the "safety valve" effect of the First Amendment is often cited as one of the values of free speech. It can also be thought of in the context of self-governing; that is, that government is best which does hear and respond to all its citizens' grievances, whatever may or may not be the violent consequences.

26. See text and endnotes at note calls 3 and 4.

27. The case is *Miami Herald Publishing Co. v. Tornillo*, 418 U.S. 241 (1974).

28. Without going into detail, and providing all the citations, some examples of the exceptions follow. (a) The "fairness doctrine" (no longer recognized by the FCC) relates to issues, not an individual's right of reply, and provides that (1) broadcasters must deal with "controversial issues of public importance," and (2) in doing so, the station cannot be used as an unrelieved instrument of propaganda; a range of views must be presented. (b) The "personal attack doctrine" provides that when a named individual is attacked by the station that individual has a right to know what was said and to personally come on the station to answer. (c) The "equal opportunity doctrine" provides that if a candidate for public office is permitted to use a station during a political campaign all other candidates for that office must be given an "equal opportunity" to use the station. (If the station owner lets no one broadcast no rights are created.) (d) Only candidates for federal office (*e.g.,* President, Senators, Members of Congress) have a right to buy a "reasonable" amount of time.

29. The leading case for this proposition is *Columbia Broadcasting System, Inc. v. Democratic National Committee*, 412 U.S. 94 (1973).

30. See discussion headed, "What are the values and consequences of the First Amendment?" above.

31. See endnote 12, above.

32. For a fuller discussion see, "What are the values and consequences of the First Amendment?" above.

33. In fact, there are a great many alternatives. Some are set forth in "Appendix: Alternative Systems of Broadcasting," below. Those described next in the text assume a system of privately owned, commercial, advertising-supported stations.

34. See discussion headed, "Who's abridging the speech?" above.

35. The Supreme Court has said, "There is no sanctuary in the First Amendment for unlimited private censorship operating in a medium not open to all." *Red Lion Broadcasting. Co. v. Federal Communications Comm'n*, 395 U.S. 367 (1969). However, that and similar language ("It is the right of the public to receive suitable access to social, political, esthetic, moral, and other ideas and experiences which is crucial here") related to a finding that the "fairness doctrine" and "personal attack doctrine" were constitutional. When it came to a right of paid entry to broadcasting the Court found there *was* a sanctuary in this "medium not open to all." That case was *Columbia Broadcasting System, Inc. v. Democratic National Committee*, 412 U.S. 94 (1973). See generally text and endnotes at note calls 27, 28, and 29, above.

36. The history of the cable industry's community access channels is too involved, and unnecessary to this paper, to explore in detail. In brief, the requirement has sometimes come from Congress, or the FCC or local city franchises. It provides that a certain number of channels (say one to six, on what are usually 20-to-60-channel cable systems) must be made available for local citizens, schools and governments. (They are sometimes called "PEG" channels, for "public, educational and governmental.") The channels are available to everyone in the community who subscribes to the cable system (at a cost of about $10 to $35 a month for all services). The usual practice is that the cable company has little or no control over the content of its "PEG" channels, and that virtually anyone can walk in off the street and put her or his videotape out over the system on the "public access channel." Although the programming on PEG channels is normally limited to a single community and cable system, and seldom has large viewing audiences, it has often played a very significant role as a showcase for local talent of various kinds, and discussion of local issues.

37. See discussion under heading, "Where the First Amendment fits in the hearts of the people," above.

38. See endnote 28, above. In fact, the Aspen Communications Program Director, Charles Firestone, once recommended an "access is fairness" proposal to the Federal Communications Commission that would have literally substituted access for the fairness doctrine. Without describing the details, the general idea was that broadcasters who were willing to make a certain proportion of their broadcast day available to uncensored speech, sometimes called "free speech messages," would no longer need to comply with the requirements of the FCC's fairness doctrine.

39. I sometimes tell the (apocryphal) story of a young reporter, who starts out with enthusiasm. She works very hard researching, interviewing, writing, and editing an "investigative journalism" article exposing the corruption of one of the major advertisers in the paper. The story is so good it may win for her a journalism prize. She proudly gives it to her editor. She never hears about it again, and it never appears in the paper. The next time she has an idea for an investigative journalism piece, about an incompetent local official, she decides to check with her editor first. He discourages her from doing the story, and she drops the idea. The third time she thinks of a major investigative journalism topic (different property tax rates paid by local citizens) she not only doesn't research and write it, she doesn't even bother talking to her editor about it. The fourth time? The fourth time the idea doesn't even cross her mind.

40. It has been estimated that as many as 60 % of the stories appearing in the *Wall Street Journal* come from publicity releases sent to the *Journal* by public relations firms on behalf of corporate clients. It is charged that some of these stories are not investigated, or even rewritten, but simply published as received.

41. Although beyond the scope of this paper, the issue of how a nation's people can be trained and encouraged to participate more actively in a national dialogue and a process of self-governance is well worth exploration. (a) Scarcely more than a generation ago the expression "children should be seen and not heard" was a common way of discouraging youngsters from speaking out. Children learn quickly from parents, and teachers, whether outspokenness is to be rewarded or punished. So adult attitudes toward children is one place to begin. (b) Opportunity is another. School newspapers, radio and television stations, training with and opportunity to use video cameras, community access channels on cable, radio and television call-in programs, and letters to the editor columns, all contribute to the opportunity for, and acceptability of, citizen participation by young and old alike.

(b) Jefferson on the Internet

This portion of chapter 1 was originally published as an article in the Federal Communications Law Journal. Nicholas Johnson, "Jefferson on the Internet," 47 Fed. Com. L.J. 281 (Dec. 1994).

Were Thomas Jefferson with us today, I am confident we would have "Jefferson on the Internet" in both senses.

Surely someone with his intellectual curiosity and inventive genius – everything from pens to plows – would have owned and used a computer and modem. Jefferson would be "on the Internet," with pithy comments scattered throughout a number of newsgroups.

But it would also be true in the sense that we would have an essay, if not a full length desktop-published volume, called "Jefferson on the Internet." In it, this advocate of free libraries, free education, and free speech would expound on the First Amendment requirements for Internet users: free and easy entry of their own information and ideas, along with access to those of others.

Of course, Jefferson is not on the Internet, and I am no longer on the Federal Communications Commission (FCC or Commission). But having spent seven years writing dissenting opinions as an FCC commissioner twenty years ago, the readers of this Journal should not be stunned to find me still at it – and still calling on Thomas Jefferson for support.

Communications technology has gone through some revolutionary changes during the intervening years, and the need for "regulation" has sometimes been altered thereby. But the basic themes and values remain, for me, unchanged.[1]

The Issue: Free Speech for All?

With the page limit on this Essay it is impossible to, as the old college essay exam question put it, "define the universe and give two examples."

So I will skip the definition, and provide only one example. It is, from my perspective, the single most important telecommunications policy challenge confronting our country: preserving the freedom of speech for all our citizens, not just those who have $200 million or more in spare pocket change to buy their own newspaper, broadcast station, or telephone company.

Let me pose the issue as a two-tiered multiple choice question: "Should telephone companies be (a) encouraged, (b) permitted, or (c) forbidden to either (1) offer conduits for information services owned and provided by others, or (2) offer information and services, which they own, through conduits which they own, in competition with the other suppliers?"

To save the reader the trouble of skipping to something called "Conclusion" (there is none) to find my answer, I will open with the conclusion, and then undertake the task of trying to persuade a skeptical, if not hostile, readership of its correctness.

I am untroubled by the first possibility: that information services over "telephone lines" may cause cable monopolists to cut rates and improve services. I am equally untroubled that cable companies – now providing a service best described as one Dixie cup and a string – are trying to enter what has been traditionally thought of as "the telephone business." I am untroubled at the prospect of others offering a continuously updated, flexibly searchable database combining what we today think of as telephone book "yellow pages" with what are now newspapers' "classified ads" – notwithstanding its modest adverse economic impact on the newspaper and telephone industries.

But I am very troubled by the second possibility: that telephone companies may soon be permitted to distribute information which they own through their own conduits.

I think it is fraudulent to argue – as the phone companies have in full page ads – that unless they own the information, then our hospitals, schools, and homes will be deprived of access to it. Almost all of the information services they hype not only can be offered by others, but *are* now being offered by others such as Mead Data Central, CompuServe, and Dialog, along with the free resources of the global Internet and the thousands of private bulletin board systems.[2] What concerns me about the common ownership of content and conduit, of course, is the telephone company's natural desire to censor and engage in anticompetitive practices.

The Natural Desire to Censor

There is a natural and almost inevitable desire to censor or otherwise use the media to support one's interests. Children are told they should be "seen and not heard." In the workplace, Peter Senge asks, "When was the last time someone was rewarded in your organization for raising difficult questions about the company's current policies . . . ?"[3]

Governments are not the only powerful institutions that try to serve their own interests through media manipulation and censorship.

My baptism by fire on this issue was ITT's proposed acquisition of ABC back in 1965-66.[4] Question: "Would ITT ever try to control ABC's coverage of the news to favor ITT's other business interests?" "Oh, no," ITT's executives would testify at hearings, and while testifying, at that very moment, their senior vice president for public relations was calling executives of the Associated Press, *The New York Times*, and the *Washington Post*, trying to change the content of the stories being filed by their reporters about that hearing! Efforts to manipulate media to serve one's other institutional interests is the most natural thing in the world.

"What are You Going to Say on the Phone?"

Imagine that we're still back in the days when AT&T owned it all. You walk into the local phone company's office and ask, "Do you have any phones? I'm new in town and I'd like a phone and a line."

The clerk says, "Well, yeah, we've got some phones."

"Can I have one?"

You get a quizzical look. "Well, just a minute now," says the clerk. "Suppose, I mean just suppose, I were to go back there and get you a phone, and get you set up with a line. What kind of things might you be planning to say over the phone?"

We either laugh or cry at that because it is so totally unimaginable. It would have been illegal, contrary to custom and experience. The phone company made lines available to anybody who wanted them.[5] And you could say anything over the phone you wanted to say. There was absolutely no censorship from the telephone company.[6]

Freedom to Speak Means Freedom to Censor

Readers of this Journal are well familiar with the *Tornillo* case.[7] The Florida legislature had passed a law that said, in effect, that

newspapers can attack politicians all they want, but when they do they
have to give the politician attacked an opportunity to respond. The
Miami Herald attacked candidate Pat Tornillo; he sought to reply
under the terms of the act; the paper refused; he took the paper to
court; he won; the paper's appeals ultimately brought the case to the
Supreme Court.

The Court found the statute unconstitutional, even though the paper
enjoyed a dominance, if not near-monopoly, throughout its circulation
area, and even though the act imposed virtually no limitation
whatsoever on a newspaper owner's right to speak her or his mind.[8]
Not only is a right of reply not constitutionally compelled, according
to the Court's interpretation, but a state legislature's provision of such
a right is constitutionally forbidden.[9] First Amendment rights belong
only to those who own the media. Their freedom to speak comes
complete with a censor's tool kit, which is certified as constitutional
by no less an authority than the Supreme Court itself. Needless to say,
that interpretation rather effectively excludes all but a relative handful
of America's 300 million citizens from meaningful participation in a
"marketplace of ideas."[10]

But this is neither the time nor the place to search for a court to which
one could appeal a Supreme Court decision, nor to draft the brief to
file once such a forum was found. *Tornillo* is the law. Moreover, it is
the law not only for newspapers, but for radio and television stations,[11]
cable television systems[12] – and even the billing envelopes of public
utilities.[13]

Freedom's Last Frontier: Free Speech by Phone

Today, the only remaining constitutionally protected free speech mass
media for ordinary citizens are telephone networks and the postal
service. Everything else has been taken from them. And once the
phone companies start providing "cable television," or other
information services they own, over the conduits they own, it is going
to be very difficult to explain why they should be denied the very same
censorship rights the Supreme Court has given to all other mass media.

Should the continuation of freedom's last frontier be left to the good intentions of phone companies? History suggests that would be dangerously naive.

Even the post office has not been immune from the natural human inclination to abuse the competitive advantages enjoyed by owners of both content and conduit. The early post offices delivered newspapers, and some of the first individuals to become local postmasters were newspaper publishers. Undoubtedly, they assured those concerned about this combination by saying: "Oh, we'll provide carriage to our competitors. Of course, we will." But it turned out they often did so at a higher rate, while delivering their own papers for free.

Next came the telegraph company. When the Associated Press was formed around the middle of the nineteenth century, there was not yet a submerged transatlantic cable. If an American newspaper wanted news from Europe, it would have to get it from Halifax, Canada, where it was obtained from ships' passengers. The New York City newspapers decided to run a telegraph line from Halifax to New York. To do that they had to use the lines of a telegraph company that served the east coast of the United States. Whereupon that telegraph owner developed a sudden desire to get into the newsgathering business himself, and refused to make his facilities available to the Associated Press.[14]

This is not a matter of ideology. It's a matter of an anticompetitive, self-serving, profit-maximizing strategy. Early in the twentieth century newspaper publishers became frightened that radio news promised to become a substantial competitor. At that point, the same newspaper owners who complained so loudly when excluded from the telegraph network saw nothing inconsistent in using all the anticompetitive political muscle at their command to keep the radio stations from broadcasting news.[15]

When motion picture production houses were permitted to own theater chains in which their own movies were shown, the anticompetitive abuses became so severe that an antitrust action was brought by the United States and sustained by the Supreme Court.[16]

Not surprisingly, when there is common ownership of both satellite programming services and the cable systems on which such programming is shown, it turns out that the cable company tends to use the jointly-owned programming and to lock out programming of competitors. In fact, the cable industry is as determined to stop the growth of home satellite receiving dishes as the broadcasting industry had earlier been to stop the development of subscription television (STV) and cable.[17]

The point is simply that abuses have occurred, are occurring, and will continue to occur when a single firm is permitted to own both the conduit through which information flows and the information itself – in competition with others also using its conduit.

The general proposition is so intuitive, and the evidence so overwhelming, that examples from within the telephone industry itself are not really necessary. Traditionally, the phone company was not in the information business, so precise precedents are hard to come by.[18] Nonetheless, the analogous abuses that have occurred reinforce the point.

Many years ago, AT&T was fighting vigorously to prevent a little microwave company from running a line from St. Louis to Chicago.[19] AT&T felt it owned it all.[20] Later that little company went by the name of MCI.

Neither AT&T nor MCI were then providing information over their networks of the kind at issue. But the analogy was that AT&T was both providing lines to its own individual customers and also providing connections and bulk lines to MCI, which MCI then resold to customers. AT&T was both MCI's conduit and its competitor, and the anticompetitive abuses in which AT&T engaged led to the largest antitrust judgment in history – $1.8 billion.[21]

It is not enough to say, "Ah, but we will require the conduit provider to make service available to those firms competing with it in the information business." It turns out that there are 10,000 ways to disadvantage one's competitor regardless of what the rules may be.[22] The opportunities are limited only by human imagination. We have seen it in the postal service, telegraph, radio and television, cable television, and telephone industries.

And even if the FCC wanted to regulate such abuses – which it doesn't – it wouldn't be able to. It has neither the will nor the resources. And if it had, Congress would quickly tell it to stop. So the only way to ensure fair competition and a diverse marketplace of ideas, in my judgment, is to prevent the merger of content and conduit in the first place.[23]

Such limitations should not be much of an economic sacrifice. Isn't it enough that telcos can suck money out of both ends of the cable – charging both information providers and recipients? In fact, I believe the case can be made that shareholders will be better off if their management is prohibited from combining conduit and content.

"Cop Killer" Telcos

Sadly, few seem to care about the concerns of public interest advocates and consumers: the fear of price hikes as telcos' monopoly services are drained to subsidize competitive businesses; the frustration over an FCC that can't, or won't, regulate; and the worries over the discouragement of innovation, censorship of content, and conflicts of interest from heavy-handed, anticompetitive telcos.

Once phone companies start exercising their First Amendment rights to speak through their own conduits, there's no reason the Supreme Court won't give them the same right to censor as newspapers and broadcasters. And at that point, the only mass medium left for those 300 million Americans who do not own their own newspaper or broadcast facility will be expensive, and relatively ineffective, direct mail via the postal service.

Given the general lack of interest in the public interest in an age of greed, and the growing gap between rich and poor, perhaps a focus on shareholder interests would be more effective in making my case.

Telco managements' interests are both clear and understandable. Adding the information business means a greater span of control and increases in executive pay and perks. It brings the excitement and glamour of socializing in Hollywood to bored, middle-aged executives.

But it turns out that shareholders may well have more in common with the creative community and consumers than with management.

Time Warner experienced enormous grief from rapper Ice-T's "Cop Killer" song. There were nationwide boycotts of the company's subsidiaries, bomb and death threats to corporate officers, the likes of Charlton Heston attacking management at shareholders' meetings. There was talk of criminal prosecutions. The creative community and the American Civil Liberties Union were equally outraged at the prospect of "censorship." And this was all from one song, on one CD, by one artist, with one record company, well down on the organization chart of this media conglomerate. A few little lyrics suddenly became a very big deal.[24]

There are thousands of such land mines lying about out there for a large corporation in the information business. Yet, controversies such as "Cop Killer" will go with the shareholders' territory once telcos provide content as well as conduit. Suddenly telcos will confront threats of defamation suits, copyright controversies, objections to obscenity – or anything thought "controversial" – and charges of censorship.

So long as telcos' shareholders insist that management stick to conduits – cables, fiber, and satellites – management can properly dismiss critics by saying, "We're just a common carrier; take your content concerns to providers, courts or legislatures. We won't oppose you or support you. We will comply with the law." In the process, shareholders will get rich beyond their wildest dreams of avarice.

But devastating and diverting adverse public relations is only the beginning.

(1) Does telco management really have the expertise, and time, to focus on information service businesses? One study reported non-phone operations were losing telcos $1.7 billion annually not long

ago.[25] Do shareholders really want more of these losses? How about a return to shareholders on telecommunications – what management is supposed to know? Adding information services makes telco executives' jobs as difficult (and senseless) as assigning one manager responsibility for administering both a virtuoso violinist and a steel mill.

(2) Are shareholders willing to take the financial bath the information businesses may offer? Motion pictures can lose, as well as make, tens of millions of dollars – even for those who know the business. More videotext and interactive businesses have gone under than prospered. Why give shareholders those headaches-and losses?

(3) Getting into the information business only heightens the risk of more antitrust grief. Is this what shareholders are looking for? Is it really worth jeopardizing the solid profits from local, long distance, and cellular data and voice telephone businesses to flirt with the risks in information?

(4) Finally, shareholders' profits are maximized by expanding capacity, and filling it with as many independent information providers as possible. With a skilled sales force, and myopic focus on that goal, profits are virtually unlimited. When telcos also sell information there's an inherent conflict. Will they make more money by selling conduit space to more providers, or by hindering them and selling the telco's own information service? Resolving that confusion only slows response time and invites antitrust suits – while reducing conduit revenues, rates of expansion, and business opportunities.

There is every reason to encourage telco provision of conduits for information providers. Everyone benefits from the competitive marketplace of ideas it creates: providers, customers, and telco shareholders.

There is every reason to oppose telco provision of information services. Everyone loses, especially the shareholders.

If telco shareholders don't want their investment to chill, while being portrayed as a Cop Killer, it's time they told management to take a sip of Time Warner's Ice-T.

Yes, however you look at it – from Thomas Jefferson's perspective, or the purposes of the First Amendment, or the needs of 300 million First Amendment-deprived citizens, or the profit opportunities of telco shareholders – separating content and conduit not only makes lots of sense, it can make lots of dollars as well.

Endnotes

1. Those "themes and values" are, quite simply, the underlying purposes, or consequences of the First Amendment: a robust "marketplace of ideas," facilitating a "search for truth," by a citizenry thereby empowered to engage in "self governing," while encouraged, through opportunities for self-expression, to "self-actualization," as they, and the more conventional media, provide a "checking value" on government and other large institutions, and a "safety valve" for those who, if denied a forum, might have chosen to express their frustrations through violence. See, e.g., *Whitney v. California*, 274 U.S. 357, 375-77 (1927) (Brandeis, J., concurring), overruled in part by *Brandenburg v. Ohio*, 395 U.S. 444 (1969); Thomas I. Emerson, The System of Freedom of Expression 6-9 (1970).

2. A classroom may not have a phone line. That's a problem. But with a computer, modem, and phone line, every student can have access to the Library of Congress and everything else publicly available to a government official or academic scientist. See, e.g., Edward A. Gargon, The Media Business, *N.Y. Times*, Oct. 6, 1994, at D20.

3. Peter Senge, The Fifth Discipline 25 (1990). Those denied opportunities for speech may find alternative means of expression. As Dr. Martin Luther King once said, "Having been denied access to radio and television we have had to write our most persuasive essays with the blunt pen of marching ranks." Dr. King believed in nonviolent solutions to grievances, but it is amazing how revolution, terrorism, or hostage-taking involves, in large part, a frustration at being silenced.

4. Compared to today's galloping global media mergers, the ABC-ITT merger looks like small potatoes indeed. But it was a big deal at the time. See In re Applications by ABC, Inc., Memorandum Order and Opinion, 7 F.C.C.2d 245, 278 (1966) (Johnson, Comm'r, dissenting), modified by Order on Petition for Reconsideration, 7 F.C.C.2d 336, 343 (Johnson, Comm'r, concurring), modified by Opinion and Order of Petition for Reconsideration, 9 F.C.C.2d 546, 581 (1967) (Johnson, Comm'r, dissenting).

5. Unlike the limited number of channels provided by today's cable companies, the phone company was required to build a new switching station whenever it came close to running out of phone lines.

6. Limitations on harassing phone calls, criminal transactions, disclosure of national security secrets, defamation, or obscenity were generally imposed and enforced by others.

7. *Miami Herald Publishing Co. v. Tornillo*, 418 U.S. 241 (1974).

8. Although the act provided for free access to the paper's pages, the Court's opinion does not hold that the result would have been different had the law provided for paid access.

9. Tornillo, 418 U.S. at 257-58.

10. Of course, it is true that thousands of citizens are heard as guests (or call-in participants) on radio and television programs, and appear in print in newspaper and magazines' "op-ed" and letters columns. As a result, at least some small proportion of the information and ideas from the general public that are supportive of the economic and political interests of media owners and advertisers will receive widespread distribution by the media. The issue is not how much of this diversity, and entry, are permitted as a matter of grace. The issue is what happens to the information and ideas of those whom media owners wish to silence. How much confrontational and controversial diversity can be distributed via the mass media over the objection of the owners as a matter of legal right? With rare exception, the answer is none.

11. *CBS, Inc. v. Democratic Nat'l Committee*, 412 U.S. 94 (1973).

12. See *FCC v. Midwest Video Corp.*, 440 U.S. 689 (1979); see also *Turner Brdcst. Sys., Inc. v. FCC*, 512 U.S. 662 (1994).

13. See *Pacific Gas & Elec. Co. v. Public Utils. Comm'n of Cal.*, 475 U.S. 1 (overturning rule requiring a utility to include in the billing envelope a consumer newsletter), reh'g denied, 475 U.S. 1133 (1986). Note that, unlike advertising-paid space, which is paid for by the speaker only if used, utility customers pay for the postage and billing envelope sent them by the utility (with its paid-for but unused space and weight) regardless of whether they are granted or denied the opportunity to use it for their own speech.

14. See Oliver Gramling, AP: The Story of News 20-30 (1940).

15. See, e.g., Erik Barnouw, A Tower in Babel 278 (1966); Sydney W. Head & Christopher H. Sterling, Broadcasting in America 160-61 (4th ed. 1982); Christopher

H. Sterling & John M. Kittross, Stay Tuned: A Concise History of American Broadcasting 122-23 (1978). With the upper hand, the newspaper publishers (normally advocates of the First Amendment's guarantees) were able to exact an agreement with the radio networks that exchanged a morsel of news from the papers for the stations' agreement to cease any newsgathering operations whatsoever.

16. *United States v. Paramount Pictures, Inc.*, 334 U.S. 131 (1948).

17. Head & Sterling, supra note 15, at 297-99, 318.

18. But see Judge Harold H. Greene's analysis of the First Amendment and other risks involved in AT&T's potential entry into electronic publishing. *United States v. AT&T*, 552 F. Supp. 131, 180-86 (D.D.C. 1982), aff'd sub nom., *Maryland v. United States*, 460 U.S. 1001 (1983).

19. Microwave Comm., Inc., 18 F.C.C.2d 953, 976 (1969) (concurring opinion).

20. It was this attitude that was made famous by comedian Lily Tomlin's great line: "We don't care. We don't have to. We're the telephone company." AT&T forbade customers to attach equipment to the telephone network if supplied by other firms. See, e.g., In re Carterphone, Decision, 13 F.C.C.2d 420, modified by Memorandum Opinion and Order, 14 F.C.C.2d 571 (1968). It even went so far as to argue that a plastic protective cover over a phone book was a "foreign attachment" with the potential to harm the quality of network service.

21. See, *e.g.*, P. L. Cantelon, The History of MCI: The Early Years 304-09 (1993); $1.8 Billion AT&T Defeat, *L.A. Times*, June 14, 1980, at 1.

22. We don't have time or space for the 10,000 examples, but here are some illustrations. The conduit provider has the lines up and operating that serve its customers, but it's going to take another six weeks before lines will be available for the competitor. The provider's lines are functioning, but the competitor's lines went down. Everybody's lines are down, but the conduit provider's are back up in 45 minutes and it takes a day for the competitor, "Because we didn't have the parts on hand." Customers can get access to the conduit provider's information in a fraction of a second, but they have to wait 20 seconds to activate the competitor's line. To connect them, the conduit provider necessarily has to be told the name and address of all the competitor's customers. What is the first thing the conduit provider's marketing department wants to do? It wants to call up the competitor's customers and try to get them to sign up, or switch.

23. Such a limitation does not, of course, prevent an individual investor from owning a small amount of stock in two separate businesses, one providing conduits and another providing the content. The limitation only applies to a single business that is engaged in both or that controls subsidiaries so engaged.

24. See Ice-T, Cop Killer, on Body Count (Rhyme Syndicate Music/Emkneesea Music 1992) ("I got my twelve gauge sawed off/I got my headlights turned off/I'm 'bout to bust some shots off/I'm 'bout to dust some cops off." Chorus: "Cop Killer, it's better you than me/Cop Killer, fuck police brutality!/Cop Killer, I know your family's grievin'/(Fuck 'em!)/Cop Killer, but tonight we get even.").

25. See Steve Sazegari, The Shape of Competition in the Local Loop, Bus. Comm. Rev., Mar. 1992, at 47.

Chapter Two: Definitional Considerations

(a) What is "The Press"?

Beginning in June 2006 the author maintained a blog at http://FromDC2Iowa.blogspot.com. This portion of chapter 2 is taken from an entry headlined, "What is 'The Press'?" August 9, 2006. The blog covered a wide variety of subjects, at least some of which involved journalism-review-type critiques of the press or opinion pieces such as this one.

In this morning's [August 9, 2006] entry, "To Riverside, With Love," I note that an earlier entry, "Caution: Wide Load, Rain Forest Ahead," August 7, "has now been expanded into a newspaper op ed column." A trivial matter by most standards, from another perspective it represents an illustration of one of those historic turning points.

What am I talking about? I'm talking about the fact that, and the way by which, a blog entry became a mainstream media column.

It turns out that some opinion page editors read blogs. One of them decided that "Caution: Wide Load, Rain Forest Ahead" might make a good column for his paper. He emailed me, and two days later there it was in print.

This, folks, is new. The bloggers have long played the role of "the people's journalism review," reading and commenting upon the mainstream media. But increasingly the flow, the interweaving of media and blogs, is going the other direction as well.

(a) The blogosphere has become a kind of mass media of its own – at least the blogs with the multi-hundred-thousand hits a day, or State 29 with 20,000 unique visitors a month (and goodness knows how many individual hits). If you consider all of our nation's 2000 conventional newspapers, there are blogs with more readers ("greater circulation") than many of those papers. At least some of the time newspaper subscribers used to spend reading papers is now spent reading blogs.

(b) For years mainstream media journalists have utilized the techniques of "investigative journalism" in discovering and reporting the foibles of major institutions. Now that bloggers are turning those very same techniques on the institution of the media itself they can no longer by ignored, as Dan Rather and CBS discovered when bloggers revealed that the "records" of President George W. Bush's military service, which CBS relied upon and reported, were fake.

(c) Mainstream media gets leads and story ideas from blog entries.

(d) Blogs aside, the Internet has now become a primary location for the mainstream media – as it has for every other institution, from agencies of the federal government, to colleges, to the Fortune 500 to small local businesses. Listen to NPR, or watch the ABC Evening News, and you're regularly referred to their Web sites where they can expand the stories and provide the background that is necessary to understanding but impossible to fit, like square pegs, into broadcasting's round holes. Advertising, from billboards to newspapers to television, often as not mentions the advertiser's Web site – a Web site that is, in effect, the company's online store, complete with a full catalog of items, as well as a means for ordering and paying for them.

(e) But the mainstream media have gone beyond merely using the Internet as a filing cabinet, or closet, to contain "all the news that doesn't fit." They have moved into the two-way communication of the blogosphere as well and are now creating their own blogs, such as the *Des Moines Register*'s blogs.

(f) And this morning (if not many times before) we have had the experience of a commercial newspaper's opinion editor selecting a column from the blogosphere to put in print.

As I prepare to teach another fall semester's "Law of Electronic Media" (at the UI College of Law) I cannot help but reflect on what it is we mean by "media" in 2006 as distinguished from what it meant 50 years ago – or even five years ago. No one fully comprehends the extent, or the implications for the future, of the convergence and changes we're living through – in terms of technologies, industries, individual and social behaviors, media formats, economics, business models, and so forth. Not the bloggers, the mainstream journalists and editors, the academics who study it – not even the multi-million-dollar-a-year corporate CEOs whose job it is to understand this stuff – no one can tell you with certainty what's happening.

When I wrote How *to Talk Back to Your Television Set* (Boston: Little, Brown, and New York: Bantam, 1970), the title captured reviewers' and readers' attention because it was so ludicrous. The mass media, television included (indeed, perhaps TV most of all) was one-way media; from one to many, with no return path. Letters to the editor and the occasional full op ed column, or audience members' calls to talk shows, were (a) a tiny sampling of the public dialogue, (b) edited and presented by the media, not by the author, up to and including, (c) the media's legal right to refuse to publish at all.

I'm reading a couple of books at the moment that take a stab at telling us readers what's happening: David Kline and Dan Burstein, *blog!* (CDS Books, 2005), and Yochai Benkler, *The Wealth of Networks* (New Haven and London: Yale University Press, 2006). They're both helpful, but neither is dispositive.

What does seem clear is that, whatever else they may have done, the Internet, Web and blogosphere have turned a from-one-to-many media environment into a from-many-to-many media environment – whatever the implications and future evolution of these changes may be.

Which brings me to the title I've put on this entry, "What's 'the press'?"

It's a reference to an exchange, of sorts, between U.S. Supreme Court Justice Potter Stewart and Chief Justice Warren Burger in the mid-1970s. Justice Stewart's salvo came in "Or of the Press," 26 Hastings Law Journal 631 (1975), a reprint of a speech he gave at the Yale Law School. The Chief Justice's response came in a separate concurring opinion in *National Bank of Boston v. Bellotti*, 435 U.S. 765 (1978).

That requires a reminder of the language of the First Amendment to the U.S. Constitution. It provides, in part, "Congress shall make no law abridging the freedom of speech, *or of the press . . .*" (emphasis supplied).

The question is, what does "or of the press" mean? Is it redundant? Did a hurried editor merely overlook the need to delete it? Did it contemplate rights regarding expression by individuals only – sometimes taking spoken form and sometimes written? Or are there two separate rights here – a "freedom of speech" for individuals and an additional set of rights, a "freedom of the press," for the institutional, corporate, mainstream media? Justice Stewart thought the latter; the Chief Justice the former.

The Chief Justice's argument was, in part, that if "the press" only refers to the institutional mainstream media – large media corporations such as the publishers of *The New York Times* and *Washington Post* – the definition excludes the only kind of "newspapers" that existed at the time the First Amendment was adopted. "The press" at that time was not that different from the "underground newspapers," or the machine copied broadsides and brochures being produced on machine copiers in the 1970s. On the other hand, if such "publications" are included as a part of "the press" there is little or no difference between "the press" and the "free speech" of individuals.

The justices' "debate" was conducted before the Defense Department's network came to be called "the Internet," and long before "the Web," with its individuals' Web pages, Facebook, and blogs. Their existence only further complicates the debate.

This blog, even if read by no more than a tiny fraction of the number of persons visiting *The New York Times'* Web site, or the *Des Moines Register*'s blogs, is no less instantaneously accessible. It uses no less a proportion of a computer screen once loaded. It and the 40 million-plus other blogs have become a source of ideas, and even columns, for the mainstream media. Meanwhile, the blogs look to the mainstream media as a source of material to comment about.

Might it not be useful for us, right about now, to take a crack at re-conceptualizing what we think is and is not "the media"? Have we created a truly new institution that is in the process of replacing what we used to think of, constitutionally, as "the press"? Or are the differences really only marginal and insignificant?

Indeed, today, "What is 'the press'"?

(b) Defining the Land of the Fourth Estate

This portion of chapter 2 was first published as "Focus: Defining the Land of the Fourth Estate," Global Issues: Media and Ethics, an Electronic Journal of the U.S. Department of State, April 2001, vol. 6, no. 1, U.S. Department of State, International Information Programs. It has been translated into Arabic, French, Portuguese, Russian, Spanish and Vietnamese.

> *"Congress shall make no law ... abridging the freedom of speech or of the press . . .."* Amendment 1, Bill of Rights, U.S. Constitution, 1791.

These words enshrine freedom of the press in the U.S. Constitution, the document that forms the structure of government and undergirds U.S. law.

In constructing the framework for U.S. government, the Constitution establishes a balance of power between the legislature, the judiciary, and the executive (the president and the administration). Each branch is imbued with separate and distinct powers that establish a system of checks and balances. The Founding Fathers painstakingly designed this governmental architecture to create a system in which the distribution of power among the branches would contribute to stability.

By the early years of the republic when this system of checks and balances was devised, a daring journalistic community had already become established. A bold and scrappy press was an influential force in denouncing the rule of an English king and leading Colonial America into its revolution against the British empire. With journalistic freedom protected in the 1791 Bill of Rights, the press became an assertive force during the first decades of nationhood. The U.S. media today is frequently known as the Fourth Estate, an appellation that suggests the press shares equal stature with the three branches of government created by the Constitution.

The Law

The presumption against regulation of the press in U.S. law can be described in a few paragraphs, but volumes have been written about the sometimes bruising and bitter struggles waged to protect press freedoms and contain the excesses of irresponsible journalism. Through it all, the independent judiciary has been an essential partner in protecting freedom of the press.

Several critical court cases have been landmarks in establishing the rights of the press to pursue information and to publish government documents or derogatory information about public figures. For instance, the U.S. Supreme Court sided with the newspapers, rather than the government, in permitting the publication of what came to be known as the Pentagon Papers. Newspapers printed these confidential Vietnam War documents, unofficially obtained, over the government's objections.

The U.S. Supreme Court also has held that the media should have some First Amendment protection from the laws of libel – lest fear of lawsuits and possible monetary damages might disincline media owners from fully reporting on public matters. In order for a public figure to win a defamation case against a media defendant, the plaintiff must show "actual malice," which the Court defined as a publisher's knowledge that the statement was false, or that he or she exercised "reckless disregard" in ascertaining whether it was false or not. *New York Times v. Sullivan*, 376 U.S. 254 (1964).

The genuine independence of U.S. federal judges is a key factor in the evolution of the legal protections enjoyed by the media. Federal judges are appointed by the president and approved by the Senate. Once in office, they remain for life, deliberately sheltered from outside pressure exerted by political interests or by executive or legislative branch officials. Judges' salaries cannot be reduced and it is virtually impossible to remove them.

Beyond these constitutionally-based principles, few, if any, laws or regulations govern the practice of journalism. The U.S. government does not license journalists or control supplies of newsprint and printers' ink. Journalists are, however, subject to the same laws generally applicable to all citizens. Newspapers, broadcast stations, and journalists must pay sales and income taxes like other businesses and citizens. Journalists are held accountable to laws regarding property trespass and highway safety just like any other citizens, no matter what their zeal to pursue a story.

The Market

Economics plays a major role in shaping the information served up to the U.S. public in newspapers, on radio and television, and now on the Internet. The media are profit-driven enterprises. While nonprofit and advocacy organizations have significant voices in the U.S. media, most of the public's primary sources of information – major urban newspapers, the weekly news magazines, and the broadcast and cable networks – are in business to make money.

The protections of the First Amendment are extended not directly to journalists who do the newsgathering, but to the owners of the media outlets through which this information is disseminated. Media owners may choose to give enormous freedom to their editors and reporters. They may consider it good business – and good journalism – to do so. But that is a matter of choice, not law. A newspaper's journalists have no more legally enforceable rights to have their stories printed than readers have rights to have their letters printed – or, for that matter, to buy space in the newspaper to promote a point of view the owner wishes to censor.

The First Amendment right to speak, the U.S. Supreme Court has ruled, includes the media owner's right to censor everyone else's speech in his or her medium. This is true even if it is the only newspaper, radio station, or TV station in town. The net effect is that the only citizens who have an absolutely unrestricted First Amendment right to disseminate their views in the press are those few who own media outlets.

Media companies are restrained from disseminating reports that reflect solely their own biases and agendas, however, by U.S. news consumers, who are capable of judging balance and accuracy in reporting among the array of journalistic products available in the information marketplace. These media-savvy citizens are quick to point out the biases and errors that appear in papers or in broadcast reports. So media owners who attempt to skew news coverage to reflect their own biases risk losing the audience, and if the audience is lost, so is the revenue from advertisers who want to reach that audience.

Newspapers, and some broadcasting networks, used to pride themselves on the "wall" between the advertising and news departments. Some critics charge that wall has been crumbling. In part this is the result of the merger of increasing numbers and varieties of media into fewer and fewer corporate hands. Detractors of this corporate consolidation fear that a network news division will no longer be accepted as a financial loss that compensates for its cost with the prestige it provides. Today, corporate boards of directors may view news as just one more "profit center," with a contributory impact on the "bottom line" and the stock price.

Balancing the cost of high quality journalism against corporate profits is one of the significant challenges in U.S. journalism today. When businesses threaten to sue over critical investigative journalism pieces or to cancel advertising, an editor or news director must decide whether to use a provocative story, even it if risks the loss of revenue or the loss of his or her own job. Thus self-censorship resulting from this dilemma, and others, may be the most prevalent form of censorship influencing the content of U.S. media today.

The Airwaves

Print and broadcast media share the same journalistic freedoms guaranteed by the First Amendment. For the privilege of using the public airwaves, however, broadcasters are subject to government regulations not imposed on their print colleagues. The Radio Act of 1927, the first law governing the broadcast medium, reflects the physical limitations of the broadcast band. Not everyone who wants to broadcast can do so because signals would interfere with one another and no service could be provided to the audience.

When national policies were being formed in the 1920s and 1930s, the United States, unlike most countries, did not choose to have stations owned and operated by a government agency or government-funded public corporation. Instead, it chose a hybrid system for the new medium. A station's equipment would be privately owned, but its right to broadcast would be regulated by government and limited by license.

The Federal Communications Commission (FCC), established in 1934, is the U.S. regulatory agency responsible for issuing broadcast licenses and for monitoring whether licensees serve "in the public interest, convenience, and necessity." In the early years, winning the privilege to hold that license required the station owner to limit the quantity of advertising and to carry a range of programming – including a large dose of news and public affairs. But aside from that, there was little, if any, interference in the content.

For the past 30 years, there has been a movement toward deregulation of broadcast media. Today the FCC imposes essentially no meaningful programming standards regarding quality or quantity. The agency has lifted earlier regulations that limited the number of stations that one owner could control in any one city, and individual corporations, which have largely replaced individual humans as the licensees, may hold licenses to hundreds of radio and television stations.

Critics allege that fewer licensees results in less diversity in broadcast programming. As corporations buy up chains of radio stations, for instance, they tend to homogenize their sound, offering less programming targeted to local audiences.

The Watchdogs

Given the central role of independent journalism in a democratic society and the absence of a constant regulator, citizens, interest groups, and journalistic associations have launched independent, nongovernmental efforts to monitor and report on media quality. None of them, of course, has any meaningful enforcement power, but they are effective in re-enforcing the principles of fairness, truth, and accuracy in reporting.

Moreover, many publications have found it useful to create the position of ombudsman – a semi-independent employee to whom readers can go with their complaints about the publication and the quality of its news coverage. The ombudsman may report on those complaints and how they were resolved in the pages of the publication.

Few institutions are more important to a democratic society than a free and independent media. Such freedom requires the public, elected officials, and civic organizations to support truth, fairness, and balance in reporting and to insist that media outlets honor the principles that empower them.

Chapter Three: Editorial Judgment and Ethics

(a) "Mr. Editor, tear down this wall!"

This portion of Chapter 3 first appeared as a blog entry, "Mr. Editor, tear down this wall!" August 8, 2006. http://FromDC2Iowa.blogspot.com.

The date was June 12, 1987. The place: the Brandenburg Gate in West Berlin. The speaker, U.S. President Ronald Reagan.

And the line we all remember from that, one of the most famous of "the great communicator's" speeches, is: "Mr. Gorbachev, open this gate! Mr. Gorbachev, tear down this wall!" Indeed, it is often referred to as the "Tear Down This Wall" speech.

The line came to me this morning [August 8, 2006] while reading *The Gazette*.

Because there's another wall that's been under attack for years and is being torn down one piece at a time – and *The Gazette* succeeded in loosening, and removing, one more brick this morning.

The wall is what once was an "Iron Curtain" in its own right, the wall between the editorial and advertising, or business, sides of a journalistic enterprise, whether print or electronic.

Indeed, though it appears quaint by today's standards, the principle is still embodied in the Society of Professional Journalists' Code of Ethics. It provides, among other things, that, "A journalist should . . . Distinguish news from advertising and shun hybrids that blur the lines between the two."

It is, admittedly, a tough standard in the context of corporate, advertiser-supported media. The most natural thing in the world for a media's CEO with little training in journalism, and a constant focus on the bottom line, would be to try to please advertisers; for an advertiser to insist that it not support financially a media outlet that runs stories attacking that very advertiser; and for a station's salesperson to want to discourage the news department from becoming such an outlet –

advocating that investigative stories be killed if necessary to avoid losing accounts.

One of the most candid – and far reaching – expressions of the advertiser's perspective is contained in a memorandum from Procter & Gamble on its broadcast policies, reported by broadcasting's preeminent historian Erik Barnouw: "There will be no material that may give offense, either directly or by inference, to any commercial organization of any sort."[1]

As the media have come to be viewed by the financial community as "just another business" – like pharmaceuticals or autos – the pressure for ever-increasing profits has resulted in layoffs of journalists, and efforts to enlist the self-interest of editors by compensating them in part like corporate executives, with bonuses and other pay based on corporate profits.

Fortunately for eastern Iowans, *The Gazette* is one of America's few remaining media outlets that is still locally owned, and therefore able to apply, when it wishes, the journalistic standards of days gone by. But even *The Gazette* lives in an ever-increasingly commercialized world, as this morning's paper revealed.

At the bottom of page one – page one! – alongside a promotional tease for a story headlined "Ultrasounds Can Affect Young Brain Development" (admittedly a story worthy of bringing to readers' attention) was another promo. This one was for a story headlined "Will New Vanilla Frosty Challenge Chocolate?" – with a prominent photo of one of those fast food drink containers clearly identified as from "Wendy's."

Normally, page one of America's newspapers has been free of ads, and reserved for the most important news of the day. Ads only appeared inside the paper. Increasingly this is changing, even by prestigious papers, up to and including the removable advertising stickers on page one with which our morning papers now arrive.

But it is the story itself which is most disturbing. Dubbed a "Food Review," this Associated Press story bylined by Casey Laughman is headlined, "Vanilla, you saucy tramp; New Frosty steals chocolate's thunder." The two columns of text bookends an even larger container with the Wendy's name, logo, and "Old Fashioned Hamburgers" clearly legible.[2]

As if the placement of this advertisement as a news story, let alone its promotion, wasn't bad enough, puffing a product that is already full of air – and goodness knows what else – the writing is really over the top. The Associated Press thinks it's important we know that Wendy's vanilla Frosties are more than "awesome," they're "uberawesome." The first taste made the journalist feel like "a chorus should be singing," from this "explosion of flavor," this "boldness . . . almost a swagger," as a result of which they are "Hooked. Bad."

But this isn't the worst of it. For some reason the author of this ad felt a need to come up with an analogy of sorts for the distinction between chocolate and vanilla. Like the ad agency that promoted "Virginia Slims" with the line, "Cigarettes are like women, the best ones are thin and rich," the analogy chosen was with women. "Vanilla would be the one to bring home to mama – safe, sweet. Works in a library. . . . Chocolate, on the other hand, is the girl in the back of the bar . . .. You know, the one with the pierced eyebrow and the tattoo on her lower back."

"Mr. Editor, tear down that wall."

"Wall? What wall?"

Endnotes

1. Erik Barnouw, The Sponsor (New York: Oxford University Press, 1978), p. 112. Barnouw notes, "The Proctor & Gamble policy statement is quoted in Green, Timothy, The Universal Eye: The World of Television (New York: Stein & Day, 1972), pp. 28-29." Ibid, p. 197, n. 12.

2. Casey Laughman, "Vanilla, You Saucy Tramp; New Frosty Steals Chocolate's Thunder," The Gazette (Associated Press), August 8, 2006 (Accent Section, p. 5D).

(b) **Local Paper Promotes Student Gambling**

This portion of Chapter 3 first appeared as a blog entry on September 26, 2006, in http://FromDC2Iowa.blogspot.com. Names of the paper, author, and students have been omitted insofar as the purpose of reprinting it here is to highlight the ethical issues rather than embarrass or indict any individual or institution.

A local paper, which has been pushing the edge of the envelope with regard to the promotion of gambling in page one stories and special supplements, ripped the envelope open this morning with a direct assault on our local high school and college youth, "Students Find New Ways to Earn Cash."

Without even a nod in the direction of balance, under a headline designed to get high school and college students' attention (after all, what student would not be interested in "new ways to earn cash"?), the paper introduces readers to a student "who plays online poker and gambles at casinos to make rent." "Gambling has paid for me to live in the last couple of years," he's quoted as saying. I'm sure many students, trying to make it on Iowa's minimum wage, will be excited to learn from the story that gambling has "proven to be much more lucrative than any regular job" for him.

Moreover, it's easy to do. "At his first casino visit, he won $600 . . . [but] still plays online three days a week." Given his gambling riches it's not surprising that "he . . . said he is considering becoming a pro poker player on the side."

But there are other ways, even if not as lucrative, for students to make money from the gambling industry. "[Another student], 21, said he found his job as a dealer at the Riverside Casino & Golf Resort through Jobnet. 'The pay is really good,' said [the student], who earns an hourly base pay of $5.50 . . . .." Yeah, $5.50 sure beats $5.15 an hour. (Actually, it's the tips that attract him.)

I've known this local paper since I've been a kid. I helped a buddy deliver the papers at one point in my life. I have read it for many of the years since. I have written regular columns for the paper during the 1980s ("Communications Watch," which was ultimately in national syndication), and 1990s (about K-12 issues, while serving on the local school board), and from time to time since. I read it early every morning with my first cup of coffee.

So it gives me no pleasure to have to criticize the paper in strong language.

But I really do think that for any paper to promote gambling in this irresponsible, inaccurate way to young people, without balance, without saying something about the real odds of winning, the real disasters it has brought into the lives of many youngsters, and the treatment programs that are available, can only be described as "shameful."

Over the past couple of months I have posted a number of blog entries on the subject of gambling and the media's promotion of the new Riverside Casino. In one, titled "Gambling's Road to Nowhere," I began:

"Nobody but the house wins from gambling; seldom do gamblers win, even in the short run and virtually never in the long run. Like a fisherman who will tell you about the big ones he caught, but seldom about the entire days spent in a boat, or on the bank, without so much as a nibble, in my experience gamblers are notoriously poor bookkeepers when it comes to recording losses with the attention to detail they bring to their winnings."

I will give the reporter – whom I have no reason to believe is anything other than an honorable, professional journalist – that the featured student actually said the things that are quoted and reported.

But were they confirmed? That even one student has found "online poker and . . . casinos" sufficiently profitable on a sustained, ongoing basis, to pay his rent and otherwise enable him "to live in the last couple years" is so outlandishly unbelievable that one would hope an editor would at least require the reporter to obtain, and share with the editor, the bookkeeping records that confirm the story.

Otherwise this is little more than a story – and a very dangerous one at that – about male college student braggadocio.

Gambling among young people is a serious problem in this country, as even a few minutes' search of the Internet will confirm. The references linked below are but a small, illustrative sampling.

The Nebraska report refers to studies by the National Gambling Impact Study Commission, the National Opinion Research Center at the University of Chicago, and the National Research Council of the National Academy of Sciences. Those studies reveal such things as that roughly one in four 18 year olds gambled in a casino during the prior 12 months, and that among the 55% of adolescents who are "casual or recreational gamblers," as many as 1.1 million kids between 12 and 18 are "pathological gamblers" – a proportion as much as three times that for adults. Moreover, quoting from an NGISC report, "pathological gambling is associated with alcohol and drug use, truancy, low grades . . . and illegal activities to finance gambling." The Nebraska paper continues, "Problems with gambling . . . increases . . . the likelihood of being involved in violent incidents [and] an increased risk for attempted suicide."

The NCAA's Director of Agent, Gambling and Amateurism Activities has testified that "The advent of Internet wagering . . . raises even greater cause for concern." He refers to the concerns of the American Academy of Pediatrics, among others:

"A 1999 Gallup Poll reports that teenagers say they start betting on college sports at age 10 and . . . at twice the rate of adults. Called 'the addiction of the '90's' by the American Academy of Pediatrics, their research indicates that there are over one million United States teens who are addicted to gambling. A recent Harvard School of Medicine report estimates that six percent of teenagers under 18 have serious gambling problems."

Not only are there adverse impacts on the youths engaged in gambling, and their families, there are costs of various kinds – including financial – to be paid by the broader community as well.

A story about the losses from youthful gambling could be a real journalistic service to any community. A story about college students' gambling as one of the "new ways to earn cash," indeed, to offset rising tuition, pay the rent and other living expenses, a substitute for what we'd normally think of as student employment, is grossly irresponsible.

Deliberate misrepresentations regarding the consequences of risky behavior, as one in a series of articles promoting gambling in general and the nearby Riverside Casino in particular, is a serious matter.

I'm not suggesting a direct parallel, and I'm certainly not urging that anyone file a law suit. But I would note yesterday's story about the $200 *billion* dollar class action suit against the tobacco companies for their misrepresentation regarding the health benefits of their "light" cigarettes. See, *e.g.*, Adam Hochberg, "Judge OKs Class-Action Suit by 'Light' Smokers," *NPR Morning Edition*, September 25, 2006.

I expect better than tobacco company ethics from my local paper.

(c) Journalist Heal Thyself

This portion of Chapter 3 is excerpted from "Retroactive Ethical Judgments and Human Subjects Research: The 1939 Tudor Study in Context," a paper prepared for delivery at the Symposium on Ethics and The Tudor Study: Implications for Research in Stuttering, Ph.D. Program in Speech and Hearing Sciences, Graduate Center, The City University of New York, December 13, 2002. It was subsequently revised and published under this title as Chapter 9 in Robert Goldfarb, editor, Ethics: A Case Study from Fluency (San Diego and Oxford: Plural Publishing, 2005).

As with the previous item in Chapter 3, the name of the reporter involved has been omitted, as the reason for this portion is only to provide an additional case study in journalistic ethics, not to indict the reporter. The article played a role in a lawsuit brought by some of the study's subjects. For a lengthy, detailed documentation of the false statements in the journalist's stories, see Defendant's Second Memorandum in Support of Summary Judgment, Nixon, et al v. University of Iowa, July 12, 2007. Among other things it reports the journalist's having prepared a letter, purporting to be from one of the plaintiffs, alleging facts known by him and the plaintiff to be false, and then obtaining her agreement "not to disclose the truth [regarding the study] to anyone." Ibid at p. 4.

Endnotes 1-6 were numbered 63-68 in the paper presented at SUNY in 2002. The expansion of endnote 5 includes the text of endnote 41 from the Goldfarb book chapter.

(Full disclosure: The supervisor of the study was the author's father.)

With all the useful newspaper feature stories that could be written about the history of either human subjects research or speech pathology, why would a reporter choose to write about a 63-year-old thesis?

It's pointless to speculate as to a journalist's motives. It does appear that there was a deliberate effort to dramatize, emotionalize, and falsely represent a 1939 master's thesis in national stories discrediting the reputation of a man 37 years dead.

This is the stuff for which the law provides remedies – such as defamation or false light. It involves the intermixture of facts both true and false to present a damaging and false overall impression of someone.

The author of the stories in question was quick to formulate and cast moral opprobrium on the researcher and supervisor. He was considerably slower in coming to an examination of his own ethical lapses. In fact, it appears he never bothered to consider them at all – from misrepresenting who he was (in violation of his paper's ethics) to dictating false statements for a plaintiff whom he then swore to secrecy (in violation of virtually anyone's ethics).

Journalistic ethics is not the oxymoron many believe it to be. There is a Society of Professional Journalists which has a "Code of Ethics,"[1] the most recent version of which was adopted in September 1996. There are a number of provisions in this Code that raise issues with regard to the ethics of the reporter's and newspaper's handling and promotion of the story about the 1939 master's thesis of Mary Tudor.

The Code speaks of goals such as "public enlightenment" from journalism. Journalists have a "duty" to "further those ends by . . .

providing a fair and comprehensive account of . . . issues. . . . [and] to serve the public with thoroughness and honesty."

"Journalists should . . . examine their own cultural values and avoid imposing those values on others."

They should "show compassion to those who may be affected adversely by news coverage. Recognize that gathering and reporting information may cause harm or discomfort . . . [and] that private people have a greater right to control information about themselves than do public officials. Only an overriding public need can justify intrusion into anyone's privacy."

Finally, a standard perhaps more applicable to the editors responsible for a newspaper's promotion, or hype, "Journalists should . . . Make certain that headlines, news teases and promotional material, photos, video, audio, graphics, sound bites and quotations do not misrepresent. They should not oversimplify or highlight incidents out of context."

Consider these admonitions in turn.

The stories detracted from, rather than added to, "public enlightenment" about ethics in human subjects research and theories regarding stuttering, and the services available to people who stutter. Their account of the issues was not fair, comprehensive, thorough, or honest.

One of the more serious indictments of the journalist's professional ethics and abilities is that the very human subject he selected to highlight was one whose fluency actually *improved* during the course of the study![2] Whatever this may indicate regarding the validity of the theory drawn from the data by the researcher, it certainly seriously undercuts the journalist's efforts to trash the reputation of Dr. Wendell Johnson because of the harm he did to the subjects. One would think that a "fair" account, presented with "honesty" would have to have, at a minimum, a measure of factual accuracy.

The stories involved the imposition of the cultural values of the journalist on others – moreover, others who lived and acted in a different time and place, 62 years before the story was written.

There was no demonstration of compassion, and total indifference to the harm or discomfort the stories would cause to the named subjects, the researcher, and the family survivors of the supervisor of the study.

There was no overriding public need that justified this intrusion into the privacy of those individuals.

In order to avoid "intrusion into anyone's privacy" at least the researcher and supervisor had enough sensitivity to refer to the subjects by number rather than by name. Unfortunately, the journalist chose to ignore both their ethical sense of decency and his own ethical standards in this regard.

The journalists' Code of Ethics also provides that,

"Journalists should . . . Avoid undercover or other surreptitious methods of gathering information except when traditional open methods will not yield information vital to the public. Use of such methods should be explained as part of the story."

On July 25, 2001, the journalist's executive editor felt obliged to run an editorial revealing that the journalist had violated the paper's own ethical standards (a provision equivalent to that quoted above).[3] The journalist had gained entry to a State of Iowa archive that is closed to journalists. He had misrepresented that his role was that of an academic researcher. The editor failed to mention any of the other ethical violations, including the violation of the privacy rights of the subjects – the protection of which was one of the purposes of excluding journalists from the archives.

As for the ethics of the promotional material, consider this promo in the journalist's paper a couple days before the series was scheduled to run. The headline blared:

"San Jose Mercury News Uncovers Secret Experiment to Make Orphans Stutter; Traces Living Legacy of Tormented Children and Haunted Researcher"

The promo began,

"In a chilling investigative series beginning Sunday, the *Mercury News* reveals for the first time the complete story of a secret experiment conducted 60 years ago to induce a group of orphans to stutter. The study [was] designed and concealed by Wendell Johnson . . .."[4]

Consider the errors and exaggerations. There was nothing to "uncover." The study was not "revealed for the first time."[5] It was not designed to create persons who stutter. It had never been secret. It was not concealed. The researcher did not "torment" the subjects. "Chilling"? "Haunted"?

As explained elsewhere in this chapter, the study was published and available in the University of Iowa library just like any other master's thesis and checked out many times. It has been described in the professional literature and by prior newspapers.

Compare this promotion with the ethical standard. Are these "headlines, news teases and promotional material [that] do not misrepresent; [that do] not oversimplify or highlight incidents out of context"? Or do they (and the series itself) have more in common with sensationalist, tabloid, supermarket scandal sheets?

The journalist's ethical violations ultimately led to his "resignation."[6] It is not within the scope of this paper to pursue whether he may also have violated legal rights referred to as defamation or false light.

It is enough to note that he is in a very weak position indeed when it comes to questioning the ethics of others – especially in the emotionally laden vocabulary of tabloid slander. After all, those he criticized acted before the existence of relevant ethical standards for human subjects research – and yet their conduct complied even with today's standards better than that of many studies in today's major institutions. He, by contrast, violated the ethical standards that were applicable to journalism at the time he wrote.

We are not looking back on his actions with the benefit of hindsight. We are not judging him with the standards of journalistic ethics at the end of their evolutionary process 63 years from now, in the year 2065. We are using the standards in place at the time he wrote, standards that presumably were well known to him.

Endnotes

Notecalls are as in original. The supporting notes are:

1. The Society of Professional Journalists' "Code of Ethics" is available online at http://www.spj.org/ethics/code.htm.

2. "As you can see, the woman 'featured' in [the reporter's] articles actually got more fluent over the four months." Dr. Robert W. Quesal, e-mail to author, June 21, 2001, with accompanying analysis of the Tudor study data.

3. Its ethics policy, violated by the journalist, provides:

"Under ordinary circumstances, reporters or photographers ought to identify themselves to news sources. There might be times, however, when circumstances will dictate not identifying ourselves. Only the Executive Editor or Editor may approve such exceptions."

To which the Executive Editor added in his editorial, "I didn't." David Yarnold, "Setting the Record Straight," *The San Jose Mercury News*, July 25, 2001.

4. The quote is from a promotional, public relations release from Patty Wise, the *Mercury News'* Public Relations Manager, distributed nationally by the PR Newswire Association, "to medical, family and features editors," June 8, 2001. It made both stories available to other papers – prior to their publication in the *Mercury News* itself, thus insuring the re-enforcing impact of the national media blitz.

5. The false claim that the study was "revealed for the first time" in the *Mercury News'* stories of 2001 is particularly ironic and unethical given that the stories' author was *himself* one of those who wrote about it earlier in the *Iowa City Mercury*! ("The Twisted Experiment of Dr. Wendell Johnson," *The Iowa City Mercury*, April 1992, p. 1.) Franklin Silverman reported on the Tudor study as early as 1988. Franklin Silverman, "The Monster Study," *Journal of Fluency Disorders*, 13, 225-231 (1988). (For a different view of the Tudor study and its media coverage from the

Silverman family see Ellen-Marie Silverman, "Paper Missed Chance to Better Inform Readers," *Milwaukee Journal Sentinel*, June 18, 2001, p. 10A: "Even more startling than the [*San Jose Mercury News*] article itself was its front-page placement and space allotment, this for an article appearing to provide no useful information whatsoever to the public . . .. How much more useful would an article about stuttering problems have been if readers had instead been informed of resources . . .. As a speech pathologist, I am particularly disheartened that the opportunity to help people prevent and treat stuttering problems was squandered in what seems to be efforts to engage in sensationalism, for what purpose or purposes one can only speculate.") The study was also the subject of a novel: Jerry Halvorson, *Abandoned: Now Stutter My Orphan* (1999) (with a forward by Franklin Silverman).

6. The AP reported the resignation. Stories that appeared in Iowa City papers included: "Stutter Story Reporter Quits," *Iowa City Press-Citizen*, July 31, 2001, p. 1, and "Author of Stuttering Series Quits Paper; Reporter Criticized for Research Method," *Iowa City Gazette*, August 1, 2001, p. 8A.

(d) Sinclair's Political Advocacy and the Public Interest

This portion of Chapter 3 consists of excerpts from an interview of Nicholas Johnson by Don Shelby on The Don Shelby Show, WCCO-AM 830, http://www.wccoradio.com, October 12, 2004. The text is drawn from a transcript of Nicholas Johnson's comments only.

A pre-2004-election controversy involved the propriety and legality (in terms of FCC and Federal Election Commission regulations of political broadcast speech) of the Sinclair station group's proposed pre-empting programming election eve to present a film attacking Democratic candidate John Kerry's objections to the Viet Nam War following his return from Viet Nam.

There are three ways of approaching what Sinclair is doing.

One has to do, not with the law as such, but just ethical behavior.

Another news story that is running today is the price gouging that is going on in regard to those who control the limited supply of flu vaccine. There is no law that prevents their price gouging, but I think most of us would agree that it is a pretty unethical, immoral thing to do.

There's no law that says a high school coach can't run up a score of 90 or 120 to nothing against an opponent, but most coaches have the decency not to do that.

Now, the second point is, there used to be laws about all this at the FCC, such as the Fairness Doctrine and personal attack doctrine. There is still the "equal opportunity" requirement for candidates in Section 315.

The FCC has now eliminated the first two. A station like WCCO follows them anyway just because it's good ethical practice, good professional journalism.

But because the rules have been eliminated by this industry-dominated FCC, the third point is that there's nothing really illegal about what Sinclair is doing in terms of FCC regulations.

Now, if this program of theirs can be considered to be a program-length political campaign commercial, the value of which constitutes a campaign contribution from Sinclair to the Bush campaign, that may well create some problem with the FEC, the Federal Elections Commission.

But in terms of the Federal Communications Commission, and the Supreme Court, they can put pretty much anything out there they want. Moreover, the Supreme Court says that with the First Amendment right to speak goes the First Amendment right to censor all others – although there are still a couple of limitations on that when it comes to broadcasting.

Now, what Sinclair is doing – essentially using their stations' media power as a force for partisan Republican propaganda – may be a gross violation of professional journalistic ethics, common decency and common sense, and so forth, but that's what we are up against.

About all you can do in a situation like this is to boycott the Sinclair stations and their advertisers. That's all these money grubbing folks who use the name "broadcaster," to the shame of the industry, that's about the only coin they understand.

What they are doing is not even ideologically driven, like a conservative talk show host. It's partisan. It's designed to help the Republican Party's candidates and hurt the Democrats.

This stands in such stark contrast to professional journalistic standards, such a clear misuse of the public airwaves, licensed to serve "the public interest."

1. There are some journalism organizations that won't even permit their reporters to go to a concert that is raising money for a candidate. Even if they are just going because they like the music. Their media organization is concerned that it might look like there was some bias or predilection to support one candidate or another. They usually let them vote, but they certainly don't let them become active in a partisan way. There wouldn't be any one of the main TV network anchors declaring their support for one presidential candidate or another. Sinclair obviously doesn't recognize those ethical principles.

2. Second, there's some "journalism," in quotes, that is just so shoddy that there's kind of no justification for putting it on the air at all. I haven't seen it, but what Sinclair is proposing to broadcast may fall into this category.

3. The other issue is, if you put on something that tends to lean one direction, then decency and good journalism would suggest you ought to put on something the other way.

That's the general idea behind the Fairness Doctrine. And, you know, I never understood why the broadcasters were opposed to the Fairness Doctrine. Most of the responsible journalists in broadcasting weren't. They found that it actually helped their cause when the advertising or sales department guy came in and said, "Look, can't you kill that documentary, because it's going to upset our advertiser. We might lose an account."

The news director was able to say, "We are required to do this by the FCC. We have to deal with controversial subjects and we have to present a range of views."

So, it helped to protect their journalistic integrity.

The Fairness Doctrine never required anything that a professional journalist wouldn't do as a matter of course. What do you do in journalism? You want controversy, you want to seek it out. And when you find it you want to present all points of view because then you've got more controversy. Even the front office should want to do it, because the more controversy you have out there the more it is going to increase the profits of the newspaper or the stations.

I never understood why the broadcasters ever opposed it. The Fairness Doctrine didn't require any particular format. It didn't require equal time. It didn't require any particular spokesperson. It didn't require they cover any particular subject, only that they cover some of the controversial issues in their community. It didn't require they put on anything in particular on the other side, just that they present a range of views and not become an instrument of propaganda.

You ask about George Soros. I'd have to say I'm troubled by big money in politics, regardless of what side it's on.

I should also say, by way of revealing my own involvement with Soros, that I have worked on projects he funds. I personally admire a guy who, in effect, not literally, but in effect spends his mornings earning billions of dollars and then spends his afternoons trying to give it all away as fast as he can. He's supporting the building of democracy in the former Soviet Republics and Eastern Europe and around the world. He's one of the most generous and public-spirited philanthropists I know anything about. So, I want to lay that on the record and disclose that.

Having said that, I'm concerned about big money in politics whether it's an individual or a corporation or a PAC of some kind. Anytime, it distorts the process. By "democracy" you mean one person, one vote. Obviously, some are a lot more equal than others, as was said in *Animal Farm*.

But you ask about the distinction between Sinclair and Soros. The distinction is that someone who sits astride the mass communication conduits in this country is in an entirely different, and much more politically powerful, position than someone who merely has the money to go beg them for time.

The law is, if I want to buy space in the *Minneapolis Star Tribune*, and they don't want to sell it to me, even though they have a rate card posted and they are taking ads from others, they have zero legal obligation to take my money and take my ad. They can thereby shut me off from the major newspaper circulated in the area – with apologies to the *St. Paul Pioneer Press*. If they both decide they don't want to let me tell the citizens of the Twin Cities what I would like to tell them, I'm silenced, I'm shut out. Now, I can go to one of these commercial copy centers and run of a bunch of 8-½-by-11 flyers and walk them around the Twin Cities and put them on everybody's doorstep, but that's scarcely a viable alternative to being able to buy space in the newspaper. And the same principle applies to radio, television, and cable television.

The Supreme Court consistently says that even though you control a monopoly media outlet or an oligopoly, one of the few major media outlets in a community, you do not have a responsibility to make time or space available to citizens in that community if you wish to censor them.

So that's an enormous distinction between the Sinclair television stations and George Soros.

Chapter Four: Media Literacy

Sailing Shark-Infested Waters: A Map for Media Literacy

This chapter first appeared in Smart TV & Sound, Winter 1997(December 1, 1997), p. 50.

Imagine yourself taking a walk in the woods. Or trying to spot a bird from the direction of its call. Or sitting on a riverbank with fishing pole in hand. Or lying on your back on the grass, watching the wind blow the leaves on the trees, and measuring the speed of the clouds. Or rolling over, and watching the purposeful daily chores of the occupants of an ant hill. These are the kinds of relaxing activities we used to call "life" or "reality." Now "going outdoors" means getting in the capsule of an air-conditioned automobile to drive on the concrete floors of the canyons between high-rise buildings. We are armchair quarterbacks, chaise-lounge travelers, virtual adventurers and couch surfers.

"Life" today, for most of us, most of the time, is a mediated existence. Our experiences are vicarious, or virtual. Most of what we know comes from media, not personal experience. Media is where politicians campaign, and then govern. It is where consumer demand is created. It's the benchmark for judging our physical appearance, popularity and "success." It encourages perspectives on race, religion, ethnicity and gender.

Think about it. How many waking hours did you spend yesterday totally isolated from all media? That means no TV, radio, music CDs or tapes, computer screens, print, or advertising signs. Were there any? If you fall asleep listening to the radio or TV, the media invade even more than your waking hours.

Media is much more than just television, but TV's influence is disproportionate. All television is "educational television." The only question is, "What is it teaching?" The average child upon entering kindergarten, for example, has already spent twice as many hours learning from television as she will later spend in a college classroom earning a B.A. degree.

Because of its pervasive and intrusive nature, television, along with newer computer-based media such as compact discs (CDs, DVDs) and the Internet, have spurred an increased demand for what the experts call "media literacy."

Sea of Manipulation

The environmental movement raised our consciousness about air quality. Still, we don't think much about breathing. We take air for granted. It's all around us. So it is with language in general and media in particular. We don't actually think about the language we use to do our thinking, nor do we actually think much about external forces that often do much of our thinking for us. We are no more conscious of the sea of symbols through which we swim than a fish is conscious of the waters of the sea.

If challenged, we respond defensively. Advertising may influence others, but we believe we are immune to its virus. And yet an honest inventory of kitchen and bathroom cabinets may reveal that multi-million-dollar advertising budgets have moved many products into our homes as well.

In fact, our brand loyalties, and the corporate logos with which we adorn ourselves (on caps, shirts, shoes), suggest we want to be known "by the companies we keep."

But irrational consumer spending may be the least risk of swimming in media-infested waters with neither map nor life jacket.

The more our lives become mediated experiences, the more difficulty we have distinguishing fantasy from reality. Soap opera stars receive gifts from fans sent, not to the actor, but to the character she plays – wedding gifts or baby presents for a wedding or birth that never really happened.

John Hinckley, who narrowly missed assassinating President Ronald Reagan, was equally confused between the actress Jodi Foster and the character she played in a movie. He assumed he could win the love of the former by carrying out the story line of the latter.

The phenomenon can touch presidents as well as their assassins. Some years ago the CBS program, "60 Minutes," did a segment called "Ronald Reagan: The Movie." It reported an academic study of the impact of feature films on the president's perceptions. For example, in a public speech he once made, Reagan attributed the award of a Congressional Medal of Honor to an act of heroism that he emotionally detailed. Later, the White House and Pentagon could not document either the medal or the heroism. It turned out the story had come from a scene in the movie, "Wing and a Prayer," which the confused President believed had actually happened. I'm not a psychiatrist, so I'm not diagnosing anyone – not Hinckley, not Reagan, and certainly not you or me. But confusing reality and fantasy can't be a sign of good mental health. Indeed, my dictionary says "a psychotic disorder characterized by loss of contact with the environment" is the definition of "schizophrenia."

The Rising Tide

As TV's influence has grown during the last forty years, a "media literacy movement" has taken root as well. Educators, public officials, parents, TV viewers, and kids themselves recognize the urgent need to create some level of public sophistication about the media and how they operate and influence us.

When I put "media literacy" into a Web search engine recently it came back with 3000 hits. Those I saw reveal there are now literally hundreds of online Web sites and list-servers, books and teaching kits, training videos, conferences and seminars, journals, magazines and organizations around the world.

And for those increasingly frequent times when parents can't share mediated experiences with their children, there is hardware like the V-chip, and software like Surf Watch, to block the most blatantly inappropriate subject matter on TV and the Internet.

"Media literacy" covers a variety of subjects. It can involve learning how a newspaper is put together, or "the language of film." It may focus on the dangers of global media monopolies. Perhaps students perform "content studies" on local TV news or newspapers. Maybe they produce local cable access video programs. Or perhaps they organize viewer protest of a local station manager or participate in an FCC rule making proceeding.

But the central aspect of media literacy is understanding the implications of the commercialization of information and entertainment. The media business is just that, a business. And, for the most part, it is not the business of selling content to consumers. Rather, it sells an audience to an advertiser at a "cost per thousand," much like cattle sold at auction at a price per hundredweight. As TV entertainer Tom Smothers once said, TV programming is like the Styrofoam in the box your toaster came in. It's there to keep commercials from rattling around and getting broken. And like Styrofoam, programming is shaped with the commercials in mind.

Advertising can be factual. Full-page supermarket ads are an example. But most national advertising is designed, like the programming packaged around it, to distort perceptions of reality. Nor is the effort limited to commercials as we typically think of them. There is also "product placement," when advertisers pay to have a product featured in a photograph, television show or feature film without identifying it as a commercial.

Advertising is often created after deep psychological probing of research subjects, which makes it easier to manipulate potential consumers. Why else would grade school girls start smoking cigarettes? Research confirms the obvious: tobacco companies' media influences them. An industry that kills 400,000 of its customers each year has to create "replacement smokers." The younger they are, the more easily and permanently they can be addicted, and the more profitable is their product loyalty during shortened lifetimes. TV programs, magazines, T-shirts, Internet sites, films and CDs can reinforce the addictive process.

Nor is the pitch limited to individual products. As I explained in a book I wrote 25 years ago, *Test Pattern for Living*, the media also sell a philosophy and lifestyle of personal identity through products – a lifestyle of hedonism, conspicuous consumption and consumerism.

Damming the Flood

So what self-defense is available? There are hundreds of suggestions in the available literature. Here are a few.

Education. For starters, become informed. Whether educator, parent, or viewer, begin to explore the media literacy resources available to you. Urge schools to start courses. Become conscious of your media environment. Talk to your friends and children about it. Try media literacy exercises at home.

News. Analyze the stories in your local paper, or local TV evening news. How much is "happy talk," weather, sports, commercials, criminal activities, trials, fires and accidents? How much is useful information, or "investigative reporting"? Are stories ever critical of major advertisers, executives of large firms, or other wealthy residents? Compare local journalism with BBC radio news, or a major newspaper from another country (many are available off the Web). What stories have your local media omitted?

Consumers. Distinguish between what you need and what some advertiser is trying to make you want. Inventory your cabinets for highly-advertised products. Can you do without? Find a generic? Do you really need all the media and communications services you're paying for? Remember your video options: over-the-air stations, cable, satellite services, video rentals. Don't like the local cable company? Cancel the service, or cut back to "basic."

Viewers. It may be the best TV is none at all. Evidence suggests that's true for kids under age eight. They need human interaction and physical activity. Plan your TV watching, and theirs, like you would theater attendance. Watch TV and Internet sites with your kids. Talk it over. Your goal should be to help them develop the standards to make their own choices – not just obey yours. Ration kids' time with TV and the Internet. Offer alternative activities.

Activists. Congress and the FCC may seem hopeless, but each is worth a postage stamp or e-mail. You can organize friends, build a coalition of local groups, and call on your local station manager, record store owner, or Internet service provider.

You wouldn't think of sailing across the Atlantic, or exploring a tropical rain forest, or driving through a big city, without a map. We're now traveling through territory that is even more alien and potentially dangerous to the human species: a "reality" that is "virtual." Road maps are available. We fail to use them at our peril.

PART TWO: "The More Things Change . . ."

Chapter Five: Media Reform

Forty Years of Wandering in the Wasteland

This chapter was originally published as one of a series of essays titled "The Vast Wasteland Revisited" in the May 2003 Federal Communications Law Journal. Nicholas Johnson, "Forty Years of Wandering in the Wasteland," 55 F.C.L.J. 521 (2003). (The star paging, e.g., *523, refers to the beginning of each page in the original.)

> *For the first time in human history we have available to us the ability . . . to furnish entertainment, instruction, widening vision of national problems and national events. An obligation rests on us to see that it is devoted to real service and to develop the material . . . that is really worthwhile.*

– Secretary of Commerce Herbert Hoover, 1924[1]

The *Federal Communications Law Journal* ("FCLJ") editors have asked us to reflect upon the changes in broadcasting's content since that fateful day, forty-two years ago [from 2003], when Federal Communications Commission ("FCC") Chairman Newton Minow challenged station owners to watch twenty-four hours of their own programming.[2]

Over the protests of a staff aide, who insisted the chairman remove the offensive "vast wasteland" phrase from his speech text, Minow persisted, ignored the advice, and is forever remembered for his two-word characterization of television programming in 1961.

Forty years later, the phrase is still with us.[3] Indeed, like other famous phrases, it has given rise to variations: "Television creates a vast waistline"; "Today television is only a half-vast wasteland." But the editors are rightly asking us for more serious reflection.

The phrase aside, what can be said about the role of television in the early twenty-first century compared with forty years ago? A candid

71

appraisal would have to conclude that it is a mixed bag. Some of the complaints about broadcasting in the 1960s are still applicable; if anything, conditions are worse. Other half-century-old complaints are irrelevant in today's media environment.

In some instances ineffective efforts at government regulation have been replaced with even more inadequate efforts at marketplace non-regulation. Today's consumers suffer at the hands of largely unregulated oligopolies.

No brief article (or entire FCLJ issue) would be long enough to cover the subject thoroughly even if the author were sufficiently informed and wise to know everything that needs to be said. But here are some observations about the changes that have occurred and what still must be done.

Shifting Sands in the Vast Wasteland

The "broadcasting" of the 1960s – as a delivery technology, commercial industry structure, and programming source – has either disappeared or assumed a far less prominent role. True, there are still transmitters and antennas sending TV signals through the air, but most Americans who "watch television" today have programming delivered to their homes through a coaxial cable or satellite dish, rather than a rooftop antenna. Viewers have choices of 50 to 100, or more channels – rather than the three networks once characterized as a "two-and-one-half network economy."[4] Much of the programming is of a kind, and from sources, that did not exist forty-two years ago, are not FCC licensees, and that distribute their programming to cable systems via satellites.

The "wasteland" critics of the 1960s have far less to complain about today in terms of number of formats, and the quantity of news, public affairs, and cultural programming. FCC Chairman Minow's efforts at increasing consumer choice were, of necessity, primarily limited to the commendable promotion of UHF stations and educational television. Put aside for the moment the issue of program quality. Clearly there are far more choices than forty-two years ago. PBS, Bravo, A&E Television, and numerous movie channels offer a range of choice of drama well beyond the episodic series of old – including a rerun of more feature films every week than Hollywood used to produce in a year. Sports are everywhere, including multiple ESPN channels. Specialty channels, from Animal Planet to the Travel Channel, further splinter while serving the audience. C-SPAN, CNN, FOX, MSNBC and CNBC – even a twenty-four-hour weather channel – offer considerably more than the fifteen minutes of evening news originally made available by the networks.

Nor are cable and satellites the only source of things to watch on TV screens. Broadcast television programming must compete for viewers' time against videotapes and DVDs. Relatively cheap (for what one gets) digital video cameras and computer video editing programs enable video buffs to make their own. There are numerous video games that can be viewed on a TV. The TV screen can even be used for surfing the Internet.

Ruminations about the implications of the Internet fill books. For now it is enough to note that: (1) time spent watching a computer screen is time not spent watching TV; (2) many of the functions of cable television, such as news, can be delivered as well or better through the Internet; (3) many TV programs (and commercials) offer a blended Internet-television service – television is a gateway to their far more detailed offerings at an Internet address prominently displayed in the TV picture; and (4) apparently a significant proportion of the audience is simultaneously watching both television and Internet-connected computer screens.

Nor is the buzzword "convergence" limited to the fact one can now watch miniature videos from a broadcaster's Web site on a computer screen or surf the Internet on a TV screen. There is coming to be less and less distinction between the handheld devices variously called cell phones, pagers, digital cameras, and Personal Data Assistants ("PDA").[5] TV screens may be as small as a wristwatch, or as large as a living room wall. The time shifting made possible by the VCR ultimately becomes a life-shifting option for families. The programs can be recorded not only on a VCR, but a computer, or a special purpose device, such as TiVo (utilizing a form of computer hard drive that may also enable viewers more easily to skip commercials).

The adverse impacts on the 1960s "broadcasters" from this competition for viewers' time have been various and dramatic. For starters, the original networks' share of sets in use is roughly half what it was then – and this for an industry that is in the business of selling the audience, as a product, to advertisers. More competitors, such as FOX, are contributing to bidding up the prices for sports and other programming. And just as newspapers had to adjust their daily product to the more rapid presentation of news, first from radio, and then from television, so yesterday's broadcasters have had to adjust their "evening news" to today's competition from cable's twenty-four-hour/seven-day-a-week news channels.

A viewer with cable reception, and a remote control device, possesses the great equalizer. Local cable access channels, low-power TV, and UHF stations (formerly beyond reception, or with clearly inferior picture quality) are now just as clear as, and only one click away from, the network affiliates – which have, thereby, lost an additional former competitive advantage.

The remote makes possible viewer choice, and program competition, with a vengeance – "entertain me now or I am gone" – in the viewer's desperate chase, constantly sampling the entirety of cable's offerings. The fear is that there may be some day, on some channel, something worth watching that the viewer will otherwise miss.

The remote, and gender differences in its use, is the subject of jokes. But its impact is no joke for those in the business who long for the vast wasteland days of a flow-through audience dutifully watching commercials. Then a viewer could be counted on to stay in his or her chair, fixed on the same station, throughout the evening. The remote means the advertiser's formerly captive audience is free to flee. Those commercials – so expensive to produce and place – may not be watched at all.

The wasteland's shifting sands make today's media landscape scarcely recognizable to a sleepy Rip Van Winkle who dozed off in front of his TV set forty-two years ago. Some things, however, have remained the same.

The Obligations, and Limits, of Capitalism

My complaints about television were in the 1960s, and remain today, not so much the harm that it continues to do (which is not trivial),[6] but the good that it fails to do.

On the one hand, we have a nation approaching 300 million persons whose memory of their education, and obliviousness to basic information, is so shocking Jay Leno has made an entertainment format out of it.[7] Most of our major health problems, and costs, come from behavioral choices wholly within the control of patients.[8] Levels of voter participation range between five and fifty percent in everything from school board to presidential elections.

Our gross ignorance of the countries and cultures of the world results in everything from "ugly American" tourists unnecessarily offending foreigners, to creating the popular apathy, or support, for military and foreign relations policies that actually provoke terrorist attacks in the United States. It impedes our ability to sell exports abroad, and requires the expenditure of billions of dollars and thousands of lives fighting wars in countries where we cannot even speak the language.[9] Nor do our television exports help those in other countries get a somewhat more accurate picture of Americans than that provided by Baywatch and Dallas.

Is television to blame for everything that is wrong in America? Of course not. Does it have the power to cure all our ills? No. Nor is this to say that programmers should provide the public nothing but an unrelieved diet of educational, public-affairs, and cultural programming. They would not stay in business long if they did. It is to say that if neither ratings nor profits need suffer from product placement, there is no reason they need suffer from information and education placement.

So on one hand we have devastating consequences from our massive ignorance and misinformation, and on the other hand we have an industry of television program producers and distributors. They have access to the minds of most American citizens for an average of some three to four hours a day. That is 80,000 to 100,000 hours over a lifetime – at least fifty times the 1800 hours students spend in college classrooms earning a bachelor's degree.

What a travesty – to be given so much access to such a huge audience, an audience with such serious needs, only to fritter it away with what Walter Lippmann once called "sideshows and three legged calves."[10] It is the difference between malfeasance and nonfeasance. It is television's having been given the power and opportunity to do such enormous good, and then failing to do it. That is the charge; that is the crime.

I continue to believe, and try to live by, the old sayings: "with great power goes great responsibility";[11] "from those to whom much has been given much is expected";[12] and "ask not what your country can do for you – ask what you can do for your country."[13]

Entrepreneurs, capitalism, advertising, profit-maximizing – and yes, "greed" – have made their contribution to our economy and lives. Some may argue that it gets a little out of hand when campaign contributors want the 1000-to-one returns on their multi-million-dollar contributions.[14] Universities now name buildings after wealthy contributors rather than revered scholars. Teens pay to wear corporate logos (rather than being paid, as was once the case, for walking the streets with advertising boards).[15] But none can question that jobs, innovations, and other benefits result when business sticks to business.

However, turning formerly non-commercial institutions over to business is one thing. Turning over the minds of America's citizens is quite another.

Cultures are shaped by their stories, their myths; self-governing societies by their ideas and information. Rather than rely on folk music, stories, and a true marketplace of the people's ideas, we have turned this public responsibility over to commerce. And commerce naturally selects those myths, ideas, and information that will provide the best media environment for commercials – and their ability to maximize hedonism, conspicuous consumption, stock prices, and the profits of an advertising-dependent media. By offering the ideas of the marketplace rather than a marketplace of ideas, we are, in effect, rotting our seed corn.[16]

That is why at broadcasting's birth there were many, in this country and elsewhere, who believed that anything with the power and potential of broadcasting should be maintained as a noncommercial enterprise.[17] At a minimum, if we are to turn our minds over to profit-maximizing capitalists, as we have, it puts an enormous burden of proof on those owners to demonstrate that capitalism, and advertising, are worthy of this most sacred trust. Am I advocating the abolition of commercial television, its nationalization, or a regulatory scheme even more detailed than that in place during the first half-century following the Radio Act of 1927?[18] No. Truth be told, even were it desirable there is very little that could be done given the political and economic power of today's media behemoths. But that does not detract from the fact that those present at the creation of American radio were right to be fearful of commercial influence in the medium, and that we have ignored their warnings to our peril.[19]

Some Modest Proposals

There is no single, innovative proposal or activity that can cure all of the media's ills. Neither is the cause hopeless. Thousands of individuals making modest progress can add up to a difference.[20]

Education in general, and media education in particular, from kindergarten through college, may be one of the best long-term solutions. Students given an opportunity for a civic education,[21] with a resulting genuine interest and participation in public affairs, may be at least a little less likely to spend hours watching "all Monica all the time" talking heads. Students accomplished in music, theater or the arts will be less likely to watch tasteless, boring, low-budget televised dreck. Those who understand manipulative advertising techniques may be somewhat less taken in by them.[22]

Citizens' media reform organizations will not win every issue. But they make a difference in keeping alive – before the agencies and in the media itself – the notion that the congressionally mandated "public interest" in broadcasting and other media means something more than mere profit maximization.[23] What are some of those issues, or proposals for reform? Here is a small sampling.

Content, Conduit, and the First Amendment

The First Amendment grants rights only to owners, not editors, not reporters, and certainly not the public. The Supreme Court makes clear that with the First Amendment right to speak goes an owner's First Amendment right to silence all others.[24] In an age when oligopolistic conduits of mass media have displaced broadsides and soapbox orators, the Court's decisions deprive more than ninety-nine percent of Americans of any right of effective speech.[25] The anti-competitive conflict of interest when a single owner controls both content and conduit – for example, cable programming sources and cable distribution systems – only makes it worse. If a proposal to totally separate content and conduit is not politically and legally viable, Congress and the FCC should at least consider restoring such minimalist requirements as the Fairness Doctrine and public service announcement requirements. Community groups' public service announcements could be selected by lottery, giving them at least a content-neutral chance to exercise their right of access to all broadcast and cable channels.[26]

Political Broadcasting Reforms

Campaign contributions are like a cancer, eating away at the vital organs of the body politic.[27] Although, there are many proposals for "campaign finance reform," in one sense there is no campaign finance problem, there is only a political broadcasting finance problem. Time buys can represent anything from fifty to ninety percent of a campaign's cost. Solve that one problem and the corrupting influence of money in politics evaporates like the morning dew. No single proposal could do more to restore the faith of a cynical citizenry than a requirement of either free time or public financing of campaigns.[28]

Ownership Limits and Diversity of Views

Congress and the FCC need to revisit, and reinstate, limits on media ownership. Problems from present ownership patterns are numerous.

Media owned by conglomerates, whether local or global, may distort their output to serve the economic interests of the parent or its subsidiaries.[29] Multiple station ownership reduces the diversity of voices. Regional concentration, or overlapping signals, creates a dangerous concentration of political power in one owner. Multiple media ownership (*e.g.*, one owner that combines control of books and magazines, and movie studios and theaters, and television stations and networks, and cable systems and programming) not only drives out economic competition, it also motivates a firm to use its subsidiaries in a self-serving, global, integrated hype of its products. This tends to promote invented superstars over the introduction of fresh and genuine talent.[30] One need not speculate as to the motives of those promoting and approving these accumulations of media power to conclude – as did members of Congress seventy-five years ago – that stricter standards are called for.[31]

Adequacy of American Journalism

No one can deny that both print and broadcast journalism can point with pride to much of quality. There are insightful portrayals of conditions both, foreign and domestic, hard hitting investigative pieces, even an occasional item exposing major advertisers. But neither can we deny that such journalism is all too rare.

Most viewers, most of the time, are at best being provided moving pictures of the headline snippets from the three or four lead stories on Reuters or the AP that day. At worst, they are watching talking (or, more likely, shouting) heads discussing ad nauseam the single, ongoing, story designed to maximize ratings[32] – if, indeed, they are watching "news" at all. News budgets are cut to the point that the more costly coverage of foreign news is limited to easily available blockbuster items – if that.[33] There is little more money for, or interest in, investigative reporting than when Walter Cronkite was complaining about its absence.[34] The range of acceptable viewpoint is extremely narrow.[35] It goes somewhere from Sam Donaldson on the "far left" to an unrelieved drumbeat of right wing conservative Republican commentators and talk show hosts on the right.

As the wall between advertising and journalism disintegrates, and editors are compensated in stock options, there is increasing pressure to provide content for none but the audience for which advertisers are willing to pay top dollar.[36]

The remedy for this national disaster of journalism in a self-governing society is not obvious. But public humiliation and shame may be a start.

Conclusion

The past near half-century has brought forth an amazing array of changes in broadcasting. Some of them, by any measure, have been positive. And yet Newton Minow had it right; and yesteryear's "vast wasteland" remains – certainly when compared to the flower garden television has the power, and refuses, to plant, irrigate and cultivate. Our "thousand points of light" have become nothing more than the glow from television sets.

Hopeless? No. But there are limits to the possible reform of the system of information and mind control we call mass media. It drives our multi-trillion-dollar consumer economy to the enormous profit of a few, and to the loss of the many. It enables the government to mobilize popular support for its wars for oil. Moreover, just as George Orwell's Winston Smith finally came to realize that, "He loved Big Brother,"[37] we have become a nation of video addicts largely beyond the power or inclination to resist.

Endnotes

1. Todd Lappin, Déjà vu All Over Again, Wired, May 1996, at 175.

2. Newton N. Minow, Television and the Public Interest, Speech Before the National Association of Broadcasters (May 9, 1961) [hereinafter Vast Wasteland Speech].

3. Indeed, as history records no special issue of a publication being devoted to the Sermon on the Mount, or Lincoln's Gettysburg Address, forty years after their delivery, this FCLJ issue may constitute an historic first.

4. One of the arguments put forward by International Telephone & Telegraph Corp. ("ITT") in its effort to acquire ABC was that it could prop up this faltering, one-half network with additional financing. The argument suffered somewhat from an internal ITT memorandum indicating the company intended to remove $100 million from ABC. Applications by ABC, Inc., Memorandum Opinion and Order, 7 F.C.C.2d 245, 321-24, 9 Rad. Reg.2d (P & F) 12, 75-78 (1967) (dissenting opinion of Johnson, Comm'r) [hereinafter ABC Memorandum]. See also Applications by ABC, Inc., Opinion and Order on Petition for Reconsideration, 9 F.C.C.2d 546, 10 Rad. Reg.2d (P & F) 289 (1967) [hereinafter ABC Opinion and Order]. See generally Karen Beth Possner, An Historical Analysis of the ABC-ITT Merger Proceeding Before the Federal Communications Commission: 1966-1967 (1975).

5. My PDA loads each morning the Web pages of CNN and *The New York Times*. Cell phones can be used to surf the Internet. Pagers can send e-mail. Other handheld devices double as digital cameras or radio receivers.

6. Here are but three examples from many that could be listed. Thousands of studies support the intuitive common sense that violence on television is more likely to encourage, than reduce, violence in real life. Many advertised foods tend to encourage, rather than reverse, what the Centers for Disease Control and Prevention characterizes as an epidemic of obesity. The televised role of women – representing a nearly impossible combination of extreme thinness and shapes like Playboy models – tends to intensify, rather than ease, the stresses young girls confront. On one hand, "anorexia nervosa . . . has increased steadily from 1975 to 1995 in 10- to 14-year-olds." Rita Melkonian, Eating Disorders in Adolescents, S.F. Med., Apr. 2001, available at http:// www.sfms.org/sfms/sfm401o.htm. "Anorexia . . . is now the third most common chronic disease in young girls between 15 and 19 years of age . . .." Id. On the other hand, "[t]he number of women and teenage girls who chose implants to augment their breast size more than doubled between 1997 and 2000" – to 203,310 in 2000 alone (exclusive of reconstruction after mastectomy). Diana Zuckerman, Are Breast Implants Safe?, Medscape Gen. Med., Oct. 24, 2001, at http:// www.center4policy.org/medscape.html. See generally Mary Pipher, Reviving Ophelia: Saving the Selves of Adolescent Girls (1994).

7. Jay Leno, host of NBC's The Tonight Show, has an occasional segment he calls "Jay Walking." He represents that he is interviewing randomly selected strangers in public places regarding basic information and understanding. The questions require knowledge of what public radio host Michael Feldman calls, during the quiz portion of his weekly radio program, "things you would have learned in school if you had been paying attention." Both features reveal a disquieting number of former (and current) students who were apparently not paying attention in school.

8. Examples might include use of alcohol and other drugs; smoking and other tobacco use; diets high in fats, calories, and sugar; lack of exercise; the availability of guns; and the failure to use seat belts and take other safety precautions.

9. Indeed, we are fighting countries we cannot even find on a map. The latest international test of students, reported while this was being written, involved thousands of students' knowledge of geography. The United States scored eighth of nine countries. Press Release, National Geographic Society, Young Americans Still In Dark on Geography, Survey Shows (Nov. 20, 2002) at http://www.nationalgeographic.com/events/releases/pr021120.html. The Swedes averaged a score of 40; the Germans and Italians, 38; the Americans, 23. Associated Press, Young Americans Flunk Geography, According to National Geographic Quiz Survey (Nov. 20, 2002), available at http://www.utsandiego.com/news/nation/20021120-1228-geographyquiz.html. Consistent with Jay Leno's results, the media's failures are confirmed both by our students' lack of general knowledge and their abundance of knowledge of television program trivia. More could locate the South Pacific island featured in the prior season's TV series Survivor than could find New Jersey on a map. One in ten could not even find the United States. Only fourteen percent of those of potential draft age could find Iraq, a country where they may be sent into battle. Id.

10. Walter Lippmann, Public Opinion 365 (1922).

11. Harry Truman, Remarks in Independence at the Liberty Bell Luncheon, Independence, Missouri (Nov. 6, 1950), at http:// www.trumanlibrary.org/trumanpapers/pppus/1950/280.htm.

12. With origins in the New Testament, Luke 12:48, Google.com indicates the phrase as quoted has been used in at least 1.4 million Web documents.

13. President John F. Kennedy, Inaugural Address (Jan. 20, 1961), available at http://www.cs.umb.edu/jfklibrary/j012061.htm.

14. For the thesis, and examples, of the 1000-to-one (or greater) payback for campaign contributions, see Nicholas Johnson, Campaigns: You Pay $4 or $4000, Des Moines Reg., July 21, 1996, at 2C, available at http://www.uiowa.edu/~cyberlaw/rcntpubl/campaign.html. The Web version contains notes to sources that were not included in the print edition.

15. As Rose Goldsen put it, "We all join in to do the work of the advertisers. We put each other in mind of their products, we call them to mind, ourselves – the greatest force of unpaid labor since the pyramids were built." Rose K. Goldsen, The Show and Tell Machine: How Television Works and Works You Over 135 (1977).

16. For but one of dozens of adverse consequences from the commercialization of information, the impact of stock option compensation on editorial judgment, see Gilbert Cranberg et al., Taking Stock: Journalism and the Publicly Traded Newspaper Company (2001).

17. Then-Secretary of Commerce Herbert Hoover's oft-quoted objection was, "It is inconceivable that we should allow so great a possibility for service [for news, for entertainment, for education] to be drowned in advertising chatter." Herbert Hoover, The Memoirs of Herbert Hoover: The Cabinet and the Presidency 140 (1952), quoted in Erik Barnouw, A Tower in Babel: A History of Broadcasting in the United States 96 (1966). Apparently the broadcasters and other members of the first Radio Conference agreed. Their Recommendation III.E. provided, "It is recommended that direct advertising in radio broadcasting service be absolutely prohibited . . .." Report of Department of Commerce Conference on Radio Telephony, Rad. Serv. Bull., May 1, 1922, available at http://www.angelfire.com/nc/whitetho/1922conf.htm. More generally, they "[r]esolved, [t]hat it is the sense of the conference that radio communication is a public utility and as such should be regulated and controlled by the Federal Government in the public interest." Id. Even "NBC visionary David Sarnoff initially thought of radio as a public service medium that should be 'untainted,' as his biographer put it, 'by money making.'" Posting of Thomas Forbes, TqDqZbjs@computerauthor.com, to x15LIN6 @computerauthor.com, at http://www.i-m.com/archives/9409/0301.html (Sept. 28, 1994) (copy on file with Journal). The Westinghouse Department of Publicity Manager came to similar conclusions. J.C. McQuiston, Advertising by Radio: Can It and Should It Be Done?, Rad. News, Aug. 1922, 232, 332-34, available at http://angelfire.com/nc/whitetho/ 1922ads.htm (last visited Feb. 26, 2003). See generally Erik Barnouw, The Sponsor: Notes on a Modern Potentate (1978), available at http://social.chass.ncsu. edu/~wiley/courses/comtech/sponsor.html (last visited Mar. 10, 2003).

18. Ch. 169, 44 Stat. 1162, Pub. L. No. 69-632.

19. See McQuiston, supra note 17.

20. The Author was involved with one such effort during the late 1970s – the National Citizens Committee for Broadcasting. Its strategies actually brought about a reduction in the levels of televised violence while it was active. See Beth Caron Fratkin, The National Citizens Committee for Broadcasting: A Forgotten Chapter of the Media Reform Movement of the 1960s and 1970s 133-49 (2002) (unpublished M.S. thesis, University of Utah) (on file with Journal).

21. For an explanation of "civic education" in social studies, see the Web sites of the National Council for Social Studies ("NCSS"), http:// www.socialstudies.org, (especially the NCSS Position Statements; Standards, Expectations of Excellence: Curriculum Standards for Social Studies, Ten Thematic Strands in Social Studies and its reference to "Civic Ideals and Practices," "Essential Characteristics of a Citizenship Education Program," and "civic participation"); and the Center for Civic Education, http:// www.civiced.org, in its entirety (both last visited Mar. 2, 2003).

22. The latest organization of media educators was announced as this was being written. See Action Coalition for Media Education, at http:// www.acmecoalition.org (last visited Mar. 2, 2003). However media-savvy one may be, a search of cupboards

and cabinets may provide illustrations of an insight Rose Goldsen once shared with the Author: "Even though we know we are being taken, we are still being taken."

23. Here are but three illustrations from the numerous national, regional, and local organizations that could be mentioned: Center for Digital Democracy, at http://www.democraticmedia.org; Center for Media Education, at http://www. cme.org; and Media Access Project, at http://www.mediaaccess.org (all last visited Mar. 2, 2003). Each Web site contains much useful information, descriptions of the organization's "issues," and links to other resources.

24. For constitutional or other reasons, the Court says this is the result for newspapers (*Miami Herald Publ'g Co. v. Tornillo*, 418 U.S. 241 (1974)), radio and television (*CBS v. Democratic Nat'l Comm.*, 412 U.S. 94 (1973)), cable television (*FCC v. Midwest Video Corp.*, 440 U.S. 689 (1979)), public utilities' billing envelopes (*Pac. Gas & Elec. Co. v. Pub. Utils. Comm'n of Cal.*, 475 U.S. 1 (1986)), and even St. Patrick's Day parades (*Hurley v. Irish-Am. Gay, Lesbian and Bisexual Group of Boston*, 515 U.S. 557 (1995)). However, the Court has recognized that the scarcity of channels for broadcast stations justifies some minimal opportunities for access, such as the Fairness Doctrine and the FCC's personal attack and political editorializing rules. *Red Lion Brdcst. Co., Inc. v. FCC*, 395 U.S. 367 (1969). Consistent congressional provisions provide all candidates an "equal opportunity" for time on any station on which their opponents have appeared (subject to numerous exceptions). 47 U.S.C. § 315 (2000). Candidates for federal office also receive a "reasonable" opportunity to buy time on stations whether their opponents have used the station or not. 47 U.S.C. § 312 (2000).

25. The distinction here is between matters of grace and matters of right. Owners may, of course, choose to publish a letter to the editor, or invite guests onto a talk show as a matter of grace. The point is that a citizen has no constitutional or other legal right to enter a mass communications conduit with a message the conduit owner wishes to censor. "Effective" is emphasized in the text because posters, handbills, doorknob hangers, telephone trees, and other options for what might be called "folk speech"–while theoretically available as alternatives – so pale in comparison with the power and reach of a message entered into a conduit of a dominant mass medium as to be almost irrelevant.

26. This would be in addition to the public, educational, and governmental (PEG) access channels on cable. Such channels serve an extraordinarily valuable purpose but do not need, and do not have, the numbers of viewers of the other channels. For a brief description of Charles Firestone's "access is fairness" proposal (*i.e.*, broadcast stations granting this type of public access could, thereby, opt out of compliance with the Fairness Doctrine), see Nicholas Johnson, Georgia's Media Future: A Personal View of Options and Opportunities, at http://www.uiowa.edu/~cyberlaw/ georgia/njtgpers.html (Mar. 12, 1998).

27. See Johnson, supra note 14.

28. That the Democratic and Republican parties are permitted to control the access of third-party candidates to the presidential debates (primarily by excluding them all, even the top one or two), through their Commission on Presidential Debates, only exacerbates the problem given those parties' limited financial resources and the crucial role of an appearance in that venue. See Commission on Presidential Debates, Candidate Selection Process, at http://www.debates.org/pages/candsel.html (last visited Mar. 2, 2003).

29. See ABC Memorandum, supra note 5; ABC Opinion and Order, supra note 5.

30. Nothing that has occurred since the "Vast Wasteland" speech lessens the concerns which the Author first published as Nicholas Johnson, The Media Barons and the Public Interest: An FCC Commissioner's Warning, Atlantic Monthly, June 1968, at 43, available at http://www.theatlantic.com/unbound/flashbks/media/johnsonf.htm (last visited Mar. 2, 2003). As explained earlier in this Essay, concerns about diversity and rights of entry are not relieved by the number of outlets or owners. The sole issue involves the rules regarding rights of entry by non-owners. The predivestiture AT&T was about as monopolistic as any communications industry could be: a single owner. The reason this raised no First Amendment issues turned on the legal rights of entry: (1) anyone who wanted a phone with access to the national network had a legal right to have one installed, and (2) could then say anything they wanted over that phone without AT&T's review of content.

31. Nearly seventy-five years ago, when the Radio Act was debated in Congress, and the miracle of radio was only barely understood, Congressman Luther Johnson of Texas was so remarkably prescient to foresee:

> American thought and American politics will be largely at the mercy of those who operate these stations. For publicity is the most powerful weapon that can be wielded in a Republic, and when such a weapon is placed in the hands of one, or a single selfish group is permitted to either tacitly or otherwise acquire ownership and dominate these broadcasting stations throughout the country, then woe be to those who dare to differ with them. It will be impossible to compete with them in reaching the ears of the American people.

67 Cong. Rec. 5558 (1926). Today it does not require prescience – only a sense of history and awareness of the evidence at hand – to know that he was right and that something must be done.

32. Examples from the past few years might include the O.J. Simpson trial, President Clinton's Monica Lewinsky affair, or the Washington D.C.-area sniper story from late 2002.

33. During the Author's term as an FCC Commissioner (1966-1973) he did a study of news programming on Japan's public network, NHK. During the sampled twenty-four-hour periods NHK not only devoted more time to news about the United States than could be found on NBC, it also provided full coverage of news from Asia, Europe – and, of course, Japan. Today many Americans seriously interested in what is going on outside their borders have abandoned American media and simply turn to the British Broadcasting Co.'s World Service, at http://www.bbc.co.uk/worldservice (last visited Mar. 2, 2003). The Author's Web page offers a link to the Web pages of numerous foreign newspapers as "a global alternative to American media." Nicholas Johnson, at http:// www.nicholasjohnson.org (last visited Mar. 2, 2003). See Nicholas Johnson, The Global Press, at http://www.uiowa.edu/~cyberlaw/ writing/glomedia.html (Nov. 12, 2002).

34. "[A]ll of them [the television networks] have third-rate news-gathering organizations. We are still basically dependent on the wire services. We have barely dipped our toe into investigative reporting." Walter Cronkite, quoted in Television: The Most Intimate Medium, Time, Oct. 14, 1966, at 57.

35. As the bumper sticker puts it, "The 'liberal media' are only as liberal as their conservative owners permit them to be."

36. See Cranberg et al., supra note 16.

37. This line is the concluding sentence in George Orwell, 1984, 226 (1949).

Chapter Six: Media Regulation and Censorship

(a) With Due Regard for the Opinions of Others

This portion of Chapter 6 was first published in the California Lawyer, Volume 8, August, 1988, pp. 52-55. The Fairness Doctrine was repealed by the FCC. Efforts to reinstate it have not been successful. The arguments pro and con have not changed much over the years.

House Commerce Committee Chairman John Dingell was livid. "I knew those lickspittles would do something like this," he said. Senate Commerce Committee Chairman Ernest Hollings shared the outrage if not the rhetoric. The action, he said, was "wrongheaded, misguided and illogical." Their comments were directed at the Federal Communications Commission, which repealed the Fairness Doctrine in August 1987.

The way for repeal had been paved by a three-judge panel of the U.S. Court of Appeals for the District of Columbia Circuit, which had ruled a year earlier that the Fairness Doctrine was an FCC directive, not a law.[1] As a result, the FCC was free to abolish the 60-year-old broadcasting doctrine by administrative fiat.

In the spring and summer of last year, Hollings led a campaign to codify the Fairness Doctrine, steering it through Congress only to be frustrated by a presidential veto. For its part, the FCC asked for comments on whether continuing to enforce the doctrine would be unconstitutional and contrary to the public interest. When congressional sponsors of a bill to save the doctrine fell eight votes short of override, the FCC acted.

Hollings still believes he can resuscitate the doctrine. And in September, the D.C. Circuit will hear arguments from supporters of the doctrine to invalidate the commission's repeal.[2] The FCC, meanwhile, is considering repeal of the Personal Attack Rule and the Political Editorial Rule, two corollaries of the fairness requirement.

What is the Fairness Doctrine, and why does anyone care about it? The doctrine requires FCC-licensed broadcasters to present programming about controversial issues, and in so doing to offer a range of views.

Its supporters include not only a majority of the Senate and House, but also many broadcast journalists and media-fearing public citizens from Ralph Nader to Phyllis Schlafly. Sixteen former FCC commissioners, who agreed to little on the commission and less since, have banded together in support of fairness.

"A range of views on controversial issues" sounds reasonable enough. Isn't that what responsible, ethical journalists do anyway? Ethics aside, isn't that the way to boost ratings?

The fight over the Fairness Doctrine is about nothing less than possession of the First Amendment: Who gets to have, and express, opinions in America. As is often the case, to frame the issue is to decide it: Where you stand is a function of where you sit.

Those who are not FCC licensees, and whose views are seldom aired, see the Fairness Doctrine as affirmative protection of their freedom, not only to contribute to the community's marketplace of ideas, but to be exposed to a wide range of views. As the Supreme Court put the argument in the *Red Lion* case:

> Because of the scarcity of radio frequencies, the Government is permitted to put restraints on licensees in favor of others whose views should be expressed on this unique medium. But the people as a whole retain . . . their collective right to have the medium function consistently with the . . . purposes of the First Amendment. It is the right of the viewers and listeners, not the right of the broadcasters, which is paramount. . . . It is the right of the public to receive suitable access to social, political, esthetic, moral, and other ideas and experience which is crucial here.[3]

On the other hand, those who have licenses are quite comfortable with controlling their stations' programming. They consider the First Amendment a negative protection from the very kind of government participation in programming represented by the Fairness Doctrine. Their views have had an impact on some economically disinterested liberals, academics and judges of varying degrees of sophistication.

Listening to these arguments, U.S. Court of Appeals Judge Skelly J. Wright of the D.C. Circuit observed in a speech, "In the current debate over the broadcast media . . . each debater claims to be the real protector of the First Amendment, and the analytical problems are much more difficult than in ordinary constitutional adjudication."

Indeed they are. Occasionally courts must balance an individual's First Amendment rights against other state interests. But how should they balance one individual's First Amendment arguments against another individual's First Amendment arguments? Perhaps we should begin at the beginning: the early days of radio.

Before the introduction of radio in the 1920s, the government had a number of communication policy options. Congress could have agreed with the Navy and let it control all broadcasting as "wireless telegraphy." It could have supported AT&T's proposal that broadcast signals become a common carrier, an idea some urge for today's cable television. It could have auctioned off frequencies to the highest bidder, or allocated stations to institutions such as universities, churches, labor unions and political parties. It could have created an American BBC or promoted viewer control.

What Congress chose was a broadcasting system in which private citizens would be licensed to use public property – the "airwaves." Broadcasters could make private profit, but only as public trustees of this valuable and politically powerful community resource. Section 301 of the Communications Act of 1934 still provides for "the control of the United States over all . . . radio transmission" and for "the use of such channels, but not the ownership thereof . . . under licenses granted by Federal authority."[4]

The government was expressly prohibited from censoring programs. But licensees would be expected to serve the public irnterest in exchange for their privileges. And regulations could minimize potential abuse.

Since 1928, among these regulations has been a cluster of policies known as the Fairness Doctrine. It is analytically useful to treat the policies individually. Some apply to candidates for political office, some to everyone and some to the presentation of issues. Some require station owners to permit the appearance of specific individuals; others merely compel the broadcast of additional material.

Section 315, the equal opportunity doctrine, often misnamed "equal time," does not require broadcasters to sell time to candidates. It triggers such rights once one candidate for a given office has been granted time. Section 312, by contrast, gives candidates for federal office a legally enforceable right to buy time regardless of circumstance. Like equal opportunity, the F.C.C.'s personal attack doctrine triggers rights in the specific party attacked. The political editorial doctrine creates comparable rights in candidates suffering the brunt of broadcasters' editorials.[5]

The general Fairness Doctrine can be traced to the FCC's 1949 *Report on Editorializing by Broadcast Licensees*,[6] and Congress' 1959 amendment to Section 315(a) requiring broadcasters "to afford reasonable opportunity for discussion of conflicting views on issues of public importance." The Fairness Doctrine's requirements are not limited to candidates or editorials, do not involve attacks, and do not trigger individuals' rights. The Fairness Doctrine only requires that broadcasters: (1) provide programs about controversial issues of public importance, and (2) in doing so, ensure that contrasting points of view are presented.

Broadcasters need not be "fair." The FCC does not designate formats, topics, scheduling or guests. There is no restriction on broadcasters' freedom to express ideas, but only on their power to censor. Fairness does not require equal balance. It does not address individual programs, only overall programming. In sum, the doctrine requires little more than what any journalist would search for anyway: stories that attract audiences and spokespersons that reflect and provoke controversy.

Most broadcast stations find it virtually impossible *not* to comply with the Fairness Doctrine. Thousands of complaints were received by the FCC from 1970 to 1978, of which 64 resulted in license revocation. Of those, only three involved fairness complaints, and each of them was decided on other grounds. In fact, since 1927 only one station has lost a license in a fairness controversy – and that decision relied more on licensee misrepresentation and deliberate violations than on an isolated fairness violation.

The FCC's present attitude toward fairness illustrates the shift from a trusteeship to a marketplace approach to broadcast regulation that began in the early 1970s. Deregulation actually began under FCC chairmen Richard Wiley and Charles Ferris. Nevertheless, the policy shift is most closely identified with President Reagan's first FCC chairman, Mark S. Fowler – characterized by critics as "the James Watt of the airwaves." In a separate statement attached to the 1985 *Fairness Report*, Fowler stated his intention to "reverse course, and head ballistically toward liberty of the press for radio and television."[7]

In 1970 and at the time of the 1974 *Fairness Report*,[8] the FCC regarded fairness as "the single most important requirement of operation in the public interest – the sine qua non." By 1985, a politically reconstituted commission saw the doctrine as probably unconstitutional, clearly not in the public interest, and unnecessary given "the multiplicity of voices in the marketplace today."

In its 1985 *Fairness Doctrine Report*,[9] the FCC concluded, "The Fairness Doctrine – in stark contravention of its purpose – operates as a pervasive and significant impediment to the broadcasting of controversial issues of public importance." But it promised to continue enforcing the doctrine, citing Congress' "intense interest" as the reason.

Until recently, few doubted the congressional and constitutional authority for the Fairness Doctrine. That the FCC should concern itself with programming was settled by Justice Felix Frankfurter's opinion in *NBC v U.S*[10].: "But the [Communications] Act does not restrict the Commission merely to supervision of the traffic. It puts upon the Commission the burden of determining the composition of that traffic." And however shocked broadcasters may have been, the 8-0 *Red Lion* decision seemed to establish the constitutionality of the Fairness Doctrine as well.

But the doctrine's moorings are coming loose in the gale-force winds from the FCC, broadcasters and political opponents. Although the Supreme Court never overruled *Red Lion*, it has given hints of wanting to distance itself from the decision. In dicta, even the *Red Lion* court suggested that "if experience" found "the net effect is reducing rather than enhancing . . . coverage, there will be time enough to reconsider the constitutional implications."

In *CBS v Democratic Nat'l Comm.*,[11] Justice Potter Stewart said in a concurring opinion that he had joined the *Red Lion* majority "with considerable doubt," and Justice William 0. Douglas added that he had not participated in the decision "and, with all respect, would not support it. The Fairness Doctrine has no place in our First Amendment regime."

The court's opinion in *Miami Herald Publishing Co. v Tornillo*,[12] suggested striking parallels to *Red Lion*'s consideration of the personal attack doctrine. A Florida statute gave political candidates a legally enforceable right of reply to newspaper attacks. State legislative candidate Patrick Tornillo sued the *Miami Herald*, which challenged the statute on First Amendment grounds, and won. The core question, said the court, was "compelling editors or publishers to publish that which 'reason tells them should not be published.'" It concluded, "The choice of material to go into a newspaper . . . – whether fair or unfair – constitutes the exercise of editorial control and judgment. It has yet to be demonstrated how governmental regulation of this crucial process can be exercised consistent with First Amendment guarantees of a free press."

If it's true for newspapers, broadcasters asked, why not for us?

In *FCC v League of Women Voters of Cal.*,[13] the court sent a double message to the FCC suggesting that it might be open to a policy shift. While recognizing the scarcity rationale, the court overturned a statute precluding public broadcasters from editorializing. But then in two footnotes the justices gratuitously raised questions about that rationale. "We are not prepared, however, to reconsider our long-standing approach without some signal from Congress or the FCC that technological developments have advanced so far that some revision of the system of broadcasting regulation may be required." The next footnote further encouraged critics, noting the FCC's suspicions that the doctrine "impeded, rather than furthered, First Amendment objectives," and adding that if "the Commission . . . decide[s] to modify or abandon these rules . . . we express no view on the legality of either course."

Despite the public interest and constitutional challenges, the statutory foundation of the Fairness Doctrine seemed secure in Section 315(a). In the *CBS* case, the Supreme Court characterized the language added in 1959 as Congress' effort "to give statutory approval to the Fairness Doctrine." But U.S. Court of Appeals Judge Robert Bork of the D.C. Circuit was not persuaded.

Siding with the commission's refusal to apply the Fairness Doctrine to teletext material in the 1986 *TRAC* case, Bork wrote, "We do not believe that language adopted in 1959 made the Fairness Doctrine a binding statutory obligation" because the doctrine was imposed "under" not "by" the Communications Act of 1934. The amendment merely "ratified the Commission's longstanding position that the public interest standard *authorizes* the Fairness Doctrine" (emphasis added). Bork also explicitly challenged the scarcity rationale, arguing that it is unclear why scarcity "justifies content regulation of broadcasting in a way that would be intolerable if applied to the editorial process of the print media." Five of the 11 sitting appeals court judges voted for a rehearing en banc, which was denied, as was a petition for certiorari.

Finally, the case against fairness was put most directly by a court in *Meredith Corp. v FCC*.[14] This was a broadcaster's appeal of a relatively routine adverse FCC Fairness Doctrine ruling (a 13:1 ratio of programming that a particular nuclear power plant was "a sound investment for New York"). The court, in remanding the constitutional question to the FCC, suggested to the commission that it might find "the doctrine cannot be enforced because it is contrary to the public interest and thereby avoid the constitutional issue."

On remand, the commission voted unanimously that the Fairness Doctrine was not only contrary to the public interest, but also unconstitutional. *Syracuse Peace Council v WTVH.*[15] What Commissioner Mark Fowler had promised six years earlier, Commissioner Dennis R. Patrick delivered. "We had absolutely no excuse, no legal reason," Patrick told *Business Week,* not to kill the doctrine.

The argument over the Fairness Doctrine continues, but still without joining of the issue.

Fairness bashers think the First Amendment protects them from government involvement of any kind. Fairness supporters say the purposes of the First Amendment require FCC procedural policies encouraging robust, wide-open debate – especially in oligopolistic communication channels. It is duplicitous, they argue, to equate FCC policies "enhancing" with those "abridging" free speech.

Although the Supreme Court in *FCC v Pacifica Foundation,*[16] relied on broadcasting's pervasiveness and impact on children as a regulatory rationale, scarcity remains the primary justification for regulating broadcasters. But in a country with only 1,600 newspapers and more than 11,000 broadcast stations, Fairness Doctrine opponents say the scarcity argument is an idea whose time has passed.

In a constitutional sense, however, there is as much scarcity now as ever. More people would like broadcast stations than there are licenses available. The licenses are still a creation of the government. The FCC still decides which bands will be used for radio and television broadcasts, which cities and licensees get them, the width of the bands, power of the transmissions and height of the antenna. And the government still sends to the penitentiary any competitor playing private enterprise on a monopolist's channel.

It doesn't sound like an open marketplace to the defenders of the Fairness Doctrine. And until the technology really does provide one, or until broadcasters share some of their license benefits, a little fairness doesn't strike advocates as much of a burden to ask in return.

Repeal of the Fairness Doctrine may be a pyrrhic victory for broadcasters. Its existence gave the audience very little. But its removal leaves a very empty place in the First Amendment that courts and Congress may now feel compelled to fill with even more effective public rights.

However it comes out, this fight is over more than what the 1928 Federal Radio Commission called "due regard for the opinions of others." It's a struggle for nothing less than possession of the First Amendment.

Endnotes

1. *Telecommunications Research and Action Center v. F.C.C.*, 801 F.2d 501 (D.C. Cir. 1987).

2. *Geller v. F.C.C.*, 867 F.2d 654 (D.C. Cir. 1989).

3. *Red Lion Broadcasting Co. v. F.C.C.*, 395 U.S. 367 (1969).

4. 47 U.S.C. Section 301 (2004).

5. 47 U.S.C. Sections 312 and 315 (2004). The F.C.C.'s "personal attack doctrine," once found as 47 C.F.R. Section 73.1920, and "political editorial rules," once found as 47 C.F.R. Section 73.1930, were repealed by the F.C.C. October 26, 2000. See, *Radio-Television News Directors Ass'n v. F.C.C.*, 229 F.3d 269 (D.C. Cir. 2000).

6. 13 F.C.C. 1246 (1949).

7. 102 F.C.C.2d 251 (1985).

8. 48 F.C.C.2d 1 (1974).

9. 102 F.C.C.2d 145 (1985).

10. 319 U.S. 190 (1943).

11. 412 U.S. 94 (1973).

12. 418 U.S. 241 (1974).

13. 468 U.S. 364 (1984).

14. 809 F2d 863 (D.C. Cir. 1987).

15. 2 F.C.C. Rcd 5043 (1987).

16. 438 U.S. 726 (1973).

(b) A Fairness Doctrine Parable

This "parable" was originally published in Hearings on S.J. Res. 209 before the Subcom. on Communications of the Senate Committee on Commerce, 91st Cong., 2d Sess. 155 (1970) (Statement of Commissioner Nicholas Johnson). It was subsequently reprinted by the U.S. Court of Appeals, D.C. Circuit, in Brandywine-Main Line Radio, Inc. v. Federal Communications Commission, 473 F.2d 16, 41-42 (D.C. Cir. 1972).

The court introduced it as follows:

"Having laid the necessary historical predicate we can turn our attention to the law of the fairness doctrine.

"The need for radio regulation has not seriously been questioned in over fifty years. As much as our historical study shows a need for this regulation, there has been a concomitant need for a fairness doctrine. America has turned away from its town meeting and processes of rural decision making. This is the electronic age-an age in which communications systems relay information to an eager public in fractions of milliseconds. Information has become the stock and trade of our informed public. So too has our method of getting information changed in the last half century. We are shifting our emphasis from the printed media to the electronic media. Radio and television consume massive portions of America's time. Because of this we must assume that the public be given access to varied information so that they may remain an intelligent and viable group-free to choose from the options available to them-free to make a choice.

"In a recent appearance before the Senate Subcommittee on Communications, Nicholas Johnson, a Commissioner of the F.C.C., expressed the need of the American people for which the Commission has undertaken to provide. This parable states the problems involved so succinctly that we reprint it in full:" . . .

Once upon a time there was a nation great in ideals and industrialization. It had businesses everywhere – and unsurpassed military might. Yet its greatest strength lay in its ideological foundation. This nation professed to be governed by the consent of its citizens. To ensure the successful functioning of this unique experiment in government, free education, libraries and full information were provided to all, so that this nation's two-hundred million governors, through wide-open debate, might govern themselves wisely. But as the years slipped by, the people spent more and more of their time in their air conditioned homes watching television, and less and less time listening to speakers in the public parks, attending town meetings, and reading handbills on the streets. Meanwhile, the number and importance of crucial issues were growing, and the need for well informed governors became paramount. Thus it was the great debate about the great debate began.

Everyone had his own theory of how to reverse this trend and return the democratic dialogue to the people, who were all at home watching their television sets. Some advocated letters, petitions, press conferences and picketing, but they had little success. Attention shifted to those who advocated bombing, burning, shooting and looting, because before and after the televising of such activities it was usually possible to present a short message, however distorted, concerning the merits of the controversy that generated such outrageous conduct. Then a third group came along. It said, "Let us simply go to the broadcasters peacefully, ask them for the time to present our concerns – we will even pay them." But the broadcasters politely explained that there was no time available for the discussion of public issues – such as war, life and politics – because the time all had to be used for programs and announcements necessary to the very difficult but essential task of inducing consumers to buy useless, joyless, and sometimes harmful products. Yet these patient and patriotic students, businessmen, and Senators were not deterred. They continued to preach the doctrine of "working within the system." "The Government," they said, "will treat us fairly. There is reason and justice in our land. Surely a democratic people need not be violent to be heard."

And so it was that they came to the Federal Communications Commission . . . .

(c) Hypocrisy and Indecency in Broadcasting

This portion of Chapter 6 is a partial transcript of an interview of Nicholas Johnson by Mike Webb on "The Mike Webb Show," KIRO 710 AM, Seattle, Washington,

March 1, 2005. This reproduction only reflects Nicholas Johnson's responses to Mike Webb's questions and comments – which can often be guessed from the responses. Mike Webb's body was found June 28, 2007, as this book was being written. I along with thousands of his other fans miss him. The Webb Web sites in 2005 were http://www.mikewebb.org; and http://www.710kiro.com.

I am happy to be with you, Mike. Thanks for the call.

Well, it seems to me that once you are paying for a service – you know, someone who has subscribed to a hard-core pornography channel on cable – that kind of removes your right to criticize the content, it seems to me. And I am not suggesting everything on cable is pornography, obviously, or indecency, but what we need to remember, is that "indecency" is an extraordinarily vague standard, so it puts a lot of power in the hands of the Administration and the FCC to frighten the broadcasters and make sure that they get favorable play for whatever the Administration's line is. Aside from the political manipulation involved in it, indecency according to the Supreme Court of the United States is protected speech.

Yes, obscenity is not protected. That can be regulated by a state legislature, a city council or Congress of the United States, and if it's regulated that would be normally be constitutional. Indecency is protected speech, but the standards vary from one medium to another. So, in over the air broadcasting, where you still have scarcity, regardless of what the critics say, and you have a license to serve "the public interest, convenience and necessity," and it's a license for a limited term, and the programming comes into the home, often uninvited, and any two-year-old can turn on the set, there is a point to having a different standard.

But, when you subscribe to cable, not to mention pay cable channels, or you subscribe to satellite radio, then it seems to me it's a little tough to be complaining.

Furthermore, when I was on the Commission, and we had some of these indecency cases, the position I took was: let's turn this over to the Justice Department. We've got laws on this and if they think it is important enough to go after, they'll do it.

When it comes to commercials, the FCC doesn't have any problems throwing up its hands and saying, "Oh, we can't do anything about that, that's the responsibility of the Federal Trade Commission." Well, if they can turn commercials over to the Federal Trade Commission, I don't know why they can't turn indecency over to the Department of Justice and have them enforce the criminal law.

The thing that troubles me about it is that it does give the FCC a kind of leverage over the broadcaster, and I think that you want to respect free speech absolutely as much as you can.

I've never been troubled by the notion of the FCC telling an over the air broadcaster that he or she needs to have something on the air in the nature of local news and public affairs. But you don't tell them what they have to put on the local news. You don't tell them they have to have the mayor on or anything like that. You say there has to something more than a jukebox with commercials.

That's another problem. The FCC has repealed the Fairness Doctrine. If you can imagine any federal agency standing up flat-footed and coming out in opposition to "fairness." Of course, the FCC also came out in favor of fraud. It used to be that fraudulent practices by broadcasters were not considered to be in the public interest, but now that's okay.

They are just throwing away all the rules, Mike.

Yes, I think if we can get Senator Stevens to be more concerned about decency towards the environment instead of drilling up there in the arctic wilderness, and then we get him one of those big, tall black hats that the Puritans used to wear, so you could see these guys coming, you see, and you would know them when you saw them.

I just think there's a lot of hypocrisy involved in this. I was watching the evening news on television earlier and here comes this woman full of sexual innuendo about Levitra. Her man gets it when he wants it, and so forth.

I would a lot rather explain about Janet Jackson's right breast to a four-year-old kid who'd been breast-fed than to try to explain to him what you have to do if you've had an erection for four hours, you know.

I mean if they want to get involved in the details of programming, which I don't think they should, but if that's what they want to do, let's take a look at the indecent commercials. Let's take a look at what the commercials are doing to young junior high girls as Mary Pipher wrote in the book *Reviving Ophelia,* and let's talk about the effort to sell illegal drugs. When you advertise pharmaceuticals on television, that's an effort to sell an illegal drug. It's illegal because the audience can't go out and buy that drug. They need a prescription.

And then all the product placement that's going on; the promotion of smoking and whatever.

If the FCC wants to get into the details of programming, I think there's a lot of stuff they can look at before they worry about indecency.

But, they don't want to do that. That's the hypocrisy. The hypocrisy is that this is a political move that's designed to serve President's Bush's base with the right wing conservative Christians. There are a lot of decent people there, and I am not being critical of them, but I mean he is pandering to them with this instead of taking a serious look at programming content.

Like you say, put the Fairness Doctrine back where we need it.

The Supreme Court took a case in which I had written a dissenting opinion as an FCC Commissioner saying that I thought if the station had time for sale they ought to be willing to sell it to everybody without making judgments about content. The Court said, "No, because we have the Fairness Doctrine, so we don't need to let people buy time."

But once you eliminate the Fairness Doctrine, then it seems to me we've got to back and take a look at the fact that in America today there are about 1500 people who have a First Amendment right to speak over the channels that make any difference. The rest of us have all been silenced. Because the Supreme Court is now saying that with the First Amendment right to speak goes the First Amendment right to censor anyone else who wants to come on your station.

Yes, there are laws involving indecency in regard to over the air stations. And Senator Stevens wants to add to that the ones you pay for: basic cable, pay cable and then the satellite radio services. And the position I have been expressing is that once you know what it is, and you've paid to receive it, you kind of abandon any right to complain about what you get. You are paying for it as much as if you went out and rented or bought a pornographic videotape or DVD.

Chapter Seven: Media Ownership and Concentration of Power

(a) The Media Barons and the Public Interest:
An FCC Commissioner's Warning

One version of this portion of Chapter 7 originally appeared as an article in The Atlantic Monthly. Another was subsequently included as a chapter in How to Talk Back to Your Television Set. It may be the most significant article written by the author during his time as an FCC commissioner in terms of its impact on the national dialogue – and the impact of the events it describes on his thinking about media ownership. The Atlantic editors described it at the time as follows: "The message aside, the medium may be turning into a quadruple threat, argues Federal Communications Commissioner Johnson. Local monopolies, regional baronies, nationwide empires, and corporate conglomerates are more and more in control of the nation's communications media – newspapers, TV, radio, magazines, books, the electronic 'knowledge industry.' The commissioner offers a brief in protest against the trend and in favor of steps to stop it. At thirty-three, Mr. Johnson already has one spirited David-Goliath role behind him: the President named him head of the Maritime Administration in 1964, where he fought for shipping industry reforms over the protests of both management and labor. He became one of the seven members of the FCC in 1966."

Before I came to the Federal Communications Commission my concerns about the ownership of broadcasting and publishing in America were about like those of any other generally educated person.

Most television programming from the three networks struck me as bland at best. I had taken courses dealing with propaganda and "thought control," bemoaned (while being entertained by) Time magazine's "slanted" reporting, understood that Hearst had something to do with the Spanish-American War, and was impressed with President Eisenhower's concern about "the military-industrial complex." The changing ownership of the old-line book publishers and the disappearance of some of our major newspapers made me vaguely uneasy. I was philosophically wedded to the fundamental importance of "the marketplace of ideas" in a free society, and a year as law clerk to my idol, Supreme Court Justice Hugo L. Black, had done nothing to weaken that commitment.

But I didn't take much time to be reflective about the current significance of such matters. It all seemed beyond my ability to influence in any meaningful way. Then, in July, 1966, I became a member of the FCC. Here my interest in the marketplace of ideas could no longer remain a casual article of personal faith. The commitment was an implicit part of the oath I took on assuming the office of commissioner, and, I quickly learned, an everyday responsibility.

Threats to the free exchange of information and opinion in this country can come from various sources, many of them outside the power of the FCC to affect. Publishers and reporters are not alike in their ability, education, tolerance of diversity, and sense of responsibility. The hidden or overt pressures of advertisers have long been with us.

But one aspect of the problem is clearly within the purview of the FCC – the impact of ownership upon the content of the mass media. It is also a part of the responsibility of the Antitrust Division of the Justice Department. It has been the subject of recent congressional hearings. There are a number of significant trends in the ownership of the media worth examining – local and regional monopolies, growing concentration of control of the most profitable and powerful television stations in the major markets, broadcasting-publishing combines, and so forth. But let's begin with a look at the significance of media ownership by "conglomerate corporations" – holding companies that own, in addition to publishing and broadcasting enterprises, other major industrial corporations.

During my first month at the FCC I studied the cases and attended the meetings, but purposefully did not participate in voting on any items. One of the agenda items at the July 20 commissioners' meeting proposed two draft letters addressed to the presidents of International Telephone and Telegraph and the American Broadcasting Company, ITT and ABC, Messrs. Harold Geneen and Leonard Goldenson. We were asking them to supply "a statement specifying in further detail the manner in which the financial resources of ITT will enable ABC to improve its program services and thereby better to serve the public interest." This friendly inquiry was my first introduction to the proposed ITT-ABC merger, and the Commission majority's attitudes about it. It was to be a case that would occupy much of my attention over the next few months.

There wasn't much discussion of the letters that morning, but I read carefully the separate statements filed with the letter by my two responsible and experienced colleagues, Commissioners Robert T. Bartley and Kenneth A. Cox, men for whom I was already feeling a respect that was to grow over the following months.

Commissioner Bartley, a former broadcaster with the deep and earthy wisdom one would expect in a Texas-born relative of the late Speaker Sam Rayburn, wrote a long and thoughtful statement. He warned of "the probable far-reaching political, social and economic consequences for the public interest of the increasing control of broadcast facilities and broadcast service by large conglomerate corporations such as the applicants." Commissioner Cox, former lawyer, law professor, counsel to the Senate Commerce Committee, and chief of the FCC's Broadcast Bureau, characterized the proposed merger as "perhaps the most important in the agency's history." He said the issues were "so significant and far-reaching that we should proceed immediately to designate the matter for hearing."

Their concerns were well grounded in broadcasting's history and in the national debate preceding the 1934 Communications Act we were appointed to enforce. Precisely what Congress intended the FCC to do was not specified at the time or since. But no one has ever doubted Congress' great concern lest the ownership of broadcasting properties be permitted to fall into a few hands or to assume monopoly proportions.

The 1934 Act was preceded by the 1927 Radio Act and a series of industry Radio Conferences in the early 1920s. The conferences were called by then Secretary of Commerce Herbert C. Hoover. Hoover expressed concern lest control over broadcasting "come under the arbitrary power of any person or group of persons." During the congressional debates on the 1927 Act a leading congressman, noting that "publicity is the most powerful weapon that can be wielded in a republic," warned of the domination of broadcasting by "a single selfish group." Should that happen, he said, "then woe be to those who dare to differ with them." The requirement that licenses not be transferred without Commission approval was intended, according to a sponsoring senator, "to prevent the concentration of broadcast facilities by a few." Thirty years later, in 1956, Senate Commerce Committee Chairman Warren G. Magnuson was still warning the Commission that it "should be on guard against the intrusion of big business and absentee ownership."

These concerns of Congress and my colleagues were to take on fuller meaning as the ITT-ABC case unfolded, a case which eventually turned into an FCC cause celebre. It also demonstrated the enormity of the responsibility vested in this relatively small and little-known Commission, by virtue of its power to grant or withhold membership in the broadcast industry. On a personal level, the case shook into me the realization, for the first time in my life, of the dreadful significance of the ownership structure of the mass media in America.

The ITT-ABC Merger Case

"ITT is a sprawling international conglomerate of 433 separate boards of directors that derives about 60 percent of its income from its significant holdings in at least forty foreign countries. It is the ninth largest industrial corporation in the world in size of work force. In addition to its sale of electronic equipment to foreign governments, and operation of foreign countries' telephone systems, roughly half of its domestic income comes from U.S. Government defense and space contracts. But it is also in the business of consumer finance, life insurance, investment funds, small loan companies, car rents (ITT-Avis, Inc.), and book publishing."

This description of ITT's anatomy is taken (as is much of this ITT-ABC discussion) from opinions written by myself and Commissioners Bartley and Cox. We objected, vigorously, to the four-man majority's decision to approve the merger. So did some senators and congressmen, the Department of Justice, the Commission's own staff, the American Civil Liberties Union, a number of independent individuals and witnesses, and a belated but eventually insistent chorus of newspaper and magazine editorialists.

What did we find so ominous about the take-over of this radio and television network by a highly successful conglomerate organization?

In 1966, ABC owned 399 theaters in 34 states, 5 VHF television stations, 6 AM and 6 FM stations (all in the top 10 broadcasting markets), and, of course, one of the 3 major television networks and one of the 4 major radio networks in the world. Its 137 primary television network affiliates could reach 93 percent of the then 50 million television homes in the United States, and its radio network affiliates could reach 97 percent of the then 55 million homes with radio receivers. ABC had interests in, and affiliations with, stations in 25 other nations, known as the "Worldvision Group." These, together with ABC Films, made the parent corporation perhaps the world's largest distributor of filmed shows for theaters and television stations throughout this country and abroad. ABC was heavily involved in the record production and distribution business, and other subsidiaries published three farm papers.

The merger would have placed this accumulation of mass media, and one of the largest purveyors of news and opinion in America, under the control of one of the largest conglomerate corporations in the world. What's wrong with that? Potentially a number of things. For now, consider simply that the integrity of the news judgment of ABC might be affected by the economic interests of ITT – that ITT might simply view ABC's programming as a part of ITT's public relations, advertising, or political activities. This seemed to us a real threat in 1966, notwithstanding the character of the management of both companies, and their protestations that no possibility of abuse existed. By 1967 the potential threat had become reality.

ITT's Empire

ITT's continuing concern with political and economic developments in foreign countries as a result of its far-flung economic interests was fully documented in the hearing. It showed, as one might expect, ITT's recurrent concern with internal affairs in most major countries of the world, including rate problems, tax problems, and problems with nationalization and reimbursement, to say nothing of ordinary commercial dealing. Its involvement with the United States government, in addition to defense contracts, included the Agency for International Development's insurance of 5.8 percent of all ITT assets.

Testimony was offered on the fascinating story of intrigue surrounding "Operation Deep Freeze" (an underwater cable). It turned out that ITT officials, using high-level government contracts in England and Canada, had brought off a bit of profitable international diplomacy unknown to the United States State Department or the FCC, possibly in violation of law. Further inquiry revealed that officers and directors of ITT's subsidiaries included two members of the British House of Lords, one in the French National Assembly, a former premier of Belgium, and several ministers of foreign governments and officials of government-owned companies.

As it seemed to Commissioners Bartley and Cox and to me when we dissented from the Commission's approval of the merger in June, 1967, a company whose daily activities require it to manipulate governments at the highest levels would face unending temptation to manipulate ABC news. Any public official, or officer of a large corporation, is necessarily clearly concerned with the appearance of some news stories, the absence of others, and the tone and character of all affecting his personal interests. That's what public relations firms and press secretaries are all about. We concluded, "We simply cannot find that the public interest of the American citizenry is served by turning over a major network to an international enterprise whose fortunes are tied to its political relations with the foreign officials whose actions it will be called upon to interpret to the world."

Even the highest degree of subjective integrity on the part of chief ITT officials could not ensure integrity in ABC's operations. To do an honest and impartial job of reporting the news is difficult enough for the most independent and conscientious of newsmen. Eric Sevareid has said of putting on a news program at a network relatively free of conglomerate control: "The ultimate sensation is the feeling of being bitten to death by ducks." And ABC newsmen could not help knowing that ITT had sensitive business relations in various foreign countries and at the highest levels of our government, and that reporting on any number of industrial and economic developments would touch the interests of ITT. The mere awareness of these interests would make it impossible for those news officials, no matter how conscientious, to report news and develop documentaries objectively, in the way that they would do if ABC remained unaffiliated with ITT. They would advance within the news organization, or be fired, or become officers of ABC – perhaps even of ITT – or not, and no newsman would be able to erase from his mind the idea that his chances of doing so might be affected by his treatment of issues on which ITT is sensitive.

Only last year CBS was reportedly involved, almost Hearst-like, in a nightmarish planned armed invasion of Haiti. It was an exclusive, and would have made a very dramatic start-to-finish documentary but for the inglorious end: U.S. Customs wouldn't let them leave the United States. Imagine ITT, with its extensive interests in the Caribbean engaged in such undertakings.

The likelihood of at least some compromising of ABC's integrity seemed inherent in the structure of the proposed new organization. What were the probabilities that these potentials for abuse would be exercised? We were soon to see the answer in the bizarre proceedings right before our eyes.

During the April, 1967, hearings, while this very issue was being debated, the Wall Street Journal broke the story that ITT was going to extraordinary lengths to obtain favorable press coverage of this hearing. Eventually three reporters were summoned before the examiner to relate for the official record the incidents that were described in the Journal's expose.

An AP and a UPI reporter testified to several phone calls to their homes by ITT public relations men, variously asking them to change their stories and make inquiries for ITT with regard to stories by other reporters, and to use their influence as members of the press to obtain for ITT confidential information from the Department of Justice regarding its intentions. Even more serious were several encounters between ITT officials and a *New York Times* reporter.

On one of these occasions ITT's senior vice president in charge of public relations went to the reporter's office. After criticizing her dispatches to the *Times* about the case in a tone which she described as "accusatory and certainly nasty," he asked whether she had been following the price of ABC and ITT stock. When she indicated that she had not, he asked if she didn't feel she had a "responsibility to the shareholders who might lose money as a result of what" she wrote. She replied, "My responsibility is to find out the truth and print it."

He then asked if she was aware that I (as an FCC Commissioner) was working with a prominent senator on legislation that would forbid any newspaper from owning any broadcast property. (*The New York Times* owns station WQXR in New York.) In point of fact, the senator and I had never met, let alone collaborated, as was subsequently made clear in public statements. But the ITT senior vice president, according to the *Times* reporter, felt that this false information was something she "ought to pass on to [her] . . . publisher before [she wrote] . . . anything further" about the case. The obvious implication of this remark, she felt, was that since the *Times* owns a radio station, it would want to consider its economic interests in deciding what to publish about broadcasting in its newspaper.

To me, this conduct, in which at least three ITT officials, including a senior vice president, were involved, was a deeply unsettling experience. It demonstrated an abrasive self-righteousness in dealing with the press, insensitivity to its independence and integrity, a willingness to spread false stories in furtherance of self-interest, contempt for government officials as well as the press, and an assumption that even as prestigious a news medium as *The New York Times* would, as a matter of course, want to present the news so as to serve best its own economic interests (as well as the economic interests of other large business corporations).

But for the brazen activities of ITT in this very proceeding, it would never have occurred to the three of us who dissented to suggest that the most probable threat to the integrity of ABC news could come from overt actions or written policy statements. After the hearing it was obvious that that was clearly possible. But even then we believed that the most substantial threat came from a far more subtle, almost unconscious, process: that the questionable story idea, or news coverage, would never even be proposed–whether for reasons of fear, insecurity, cynicism, realism, or unconscious avoidance.

Concentration of Control Over the Media

Since the ITT-ABC case left the Commission I have not ceased to be troubled by the issues it raised – in many ways more serious (and certainly more prevalent) for wholly domestic corporations. Eventually the merger was aborted by ITT on New Year's Day of this year, while the Justice Department's appeal of the Commission's action was pending before the U.S. Court of Appeals. However, I ponder what the consequences might have been if ITT's apparent cynicism toward journalistic integrity had actually been able to harness the enormous social and propaganda power of a national television network to the service of a politically sensitive corporate conglomerate. More important, I have become concerned about the extent to which such forces already play upon important media of mass communication. Perhaps such attitudes are masked by more finesse than that displayed in the ITT-ABC case. Perhaps they are even embedded in the kind of sincere good intentions which caused former Defense Secretary (and former General Motors president) Charles Wilson to equate the interests of his company with those of the country.

I do not believe that most owners and managers of the mass media in the United States lack a sense of responsibility or lack tolerance for a diversity of views. I do not believe there is a small group of men who gather for breakfast every morning and decide what they will make the American people believe that day. Emotion often outruns the evidence of those who argue a conspiracy theory of propagandists' manipulation of the masses.

On the other hand, one reason evidence is so hard to come by is that the media tend to give less publicity to their own abuses than, say, to those of politicians. The media operate as a check upon other institutional power centers in our country. There is, however, no check upon the media. Just as it is a mistake to overstate the existence and potential for abuse, so, in my judgment, is it a mistake to ignore the evidence that does exist.

In 1959, for example, it was reported that officials of the Trujillo regime in the Dominican Republic had paid $750,000 to officers of the

Mutual Radio Network to gain favorable propaganda disguised as news. (Ownership of the Mutual Radio Network changed hands once again last year without any review whatsoever by the FCC of old or new owners. The FCC does not regulate networks, only stations and Mutual owns none.) RCA was once charged with using an NBC station to serve unfairly its broader corporate interests, including the coverage of RCA activities as "news," when others did not. There was speculation that after RCA acquired Random House, considerable pressure was put on the book publishing house's president, Bennett Cerf, to cease his Sunday evening service as a panelist on CBS's What's My Line? The Commission has occasionally found that individual stations have violated the "fairness doctrine" in advocating causes serving the station's economic self-interest, such as pay television.

Virtually every issue of the *Columbia Journalism Review* reports instances of such abuses by the print media. It has described a railroad-owned newspaper that refused to report railroad wrecks, a newspaper in debt to the Teamsters Union which gave exceedingly favorable coverage to Jimmy Hoffa, the repeated influence of the DuPont interests in the editorial functions of the Wilmington papers which it owned, and Anaconda Copper's use of its company-owned newspapers to support political candidates favorable to the company.

Edward P. Morgan left ABC last year to become the commentator on the Ford Foundation-funded Public Broadcasting Laboratory. He has always been straightforward, and he used his final news broadcast to be reflective about broadcasting itself. "Let's face it," he said. "We in this trade use this power more frequently to fix a traffic ticket or get a ticket to a ballgame than to keep the doors of an open society open and swinging . . .. The freest and most profitable press in the world, every major facet of it, not only ducks but pulls its punches to save a supermarket of commercialism or shield an ugly prejudice and is putting the life of the republic in jeopardy thereby."

Economic self-interest does influence the content of the media, and as the media tend to fall into the control of corporate conglomerates, the areas of information and opinion affecting those economic interests become dangerously wide-ranging. What is happening to the ownership of American media today? What dangers does it pose? Taking a look at the structure of the media in the United States, I am not put at ease by what I see.

Most American communities have far less "dissemination of information from diverse and antagonistic sources" (to quote a famous description by the Supreme Court of the basic aim of the First Amendment) than is available nationally. Of the 1500 cities with daily newspapers, 96 percent are served by single-owner monopolies. Outside the top 50 to 200 markets there is a substantial dropping off in the number of competing radio and television signals. The FCC prohibits a single owner from controlling two AM radio, or two television, stations with overlapping signals. But it has only recently expressed any concern over common ownership of an AM radio station and an FM radio station and a television station in the same market. Indeed, such ownership is the rule rather than the exception and probably exists in your community. Most stations are today acquired by purchase. And the FCC has, in part because of congressional pressure, rarely disapproved a purchase of a station by a newspaper.

There are few statewide or regional "monopolies" – although some situations come close. But in a majority of our states – the least populous – there are few enough newspapers and television stations to begin with, and they are usually under the control of a small group. And most politicians find today, as Congress warned in 1926, "woe be to those who dare to differ with them." Most of our politics is still state and local in scope. And increasingly, in many states and local communities, congressmen and state and local officials are compelled to regard that handful of media owners (many of whom are out-of-state), rather than the electorate itself, as their effective constituency. Moreover, many mass media owners have a significant impact in more than one state. One case that came before the FCC, for example, involved an owner with AM-FM-TV combinations in Las Vegas and Reno, Nevada, along with four newspapers in that state, seven newspapers in Oklahoma, and two stations and two newspapers in Arkansas. Another involved ownership of ten stations in North Carolina and adjoining southern Virginia. You may never have heard of these owners, but I imagine the elected officials of their states return their phone calls promptly.

National Power

The principal national sources of news are the wire services, AP and UPI, and the broadcast networks. Each of the wire services serves on the order of 1200 newspapers and 3000 radio and television stations. Most local newspapers and radio stations offer little more than wire service copy as far as national and international news is concerned. To that extent one can take little heart for "diversity" from the oft-proffered statistics on proliferating radio stations (now over 6000) and the remaining daily newspapers (1700). The networks, though themselves heavily reliant upon the wire services to find out what's worth filming, are another potent force.

The weekly newsmagazine field is dominated by *Time*, *Newsweek*, and *U.S. News*. The first two also control substantial broadcast, newspaper, and book or publishing outlets. Time is also in movies (MGM) and is hungry for three or four newspapers. Thus, even though there are thousands of general and specialized periodicals and program sources with significant national or regional impact, and certainly no "monopoly" exists, it is still possible for a single individual or corporation to have vast national influence.

What we sometimes fail to realize, moreover, is the political significance of the fact that we have become a nation of cities. Nearly half of the American people live in the six largest states: California, New York, Illinois, Pennsylvania, Texas, and Ohio. Those states, in turn, are substantially influenced (if not politically dominated) by their major population-industrial-financial-media centers, such as Los Angeles, New York City, Chicago, and Philadelphia – the nation's four largest metropolitan areas. Thus, to have a major newspaper or television station influence in one of these cities is to have significant national power. And the number of interests with influence in more than one of these markets is startling.

Most of the top fifty television markets (which serve approximately 75 percent of the nation's television homes) have three competing commercial VHF television stations. There are about 150 such VHF commercial stations in these markets. Less than 10 percent are today owned by entities that do not own other media interests. In 30 of the 50 markets at least one of the stations is owned by a major newspaper published in that market – a total of one third of these 150 stations. In Dallas-Fort Worth each of the network affiliates is owned by a local newspaper, and the fourth, an unaffiliated station, is owned by Oklahoma newspapers. Moreover, half of the newspaper-owned stations are controlled by seven groups – groups that also publish magazines as popular and diverse as *Time, Newsweek, Look, Parade, Harper's, TV Guide, Family Circle, Vogue, Good Housekeeping*, and *Popular Mechanics*. Twelve parties own more than one third of all the major-market stations.

In addition to the vast national impact of their affiliates the three television networks each own VHF stations in all of the top three markets – New York, Los Angeles, and Chicago – and each has two more in other cities in the top ten. RKO and Metromedia each own stations in both New York City and Los Angeles. Metromedia also owns stations in Washington, D.C., and California's other major city, San Francisco – as well as Philadelphia, Baltimore, Cleveland, Kansas City, and Oakland. RKO also owns stations in Boston, San Francisco, Washington, Memphis, Hartford, and Windsor, Ontario – as well as the regional Yankee Network. Westinghouse owns stations in New York, Chicago, Philadelphia and Pittsburgh, Pennsylvania, Boston, San Francisco, Baltimore, and Fort Wayne. These are but a few examples of today's media barons.

There are many implications of their power. Groups of stations are able to bargain with networks, advertisers, and talent in ways that put lesser stations at substantial economic disadvantage. Group ownership means, by definition, that few stations in major markets will be locally owned. The FCC recently approved the transfer of the last available station in San Francisco to the absentee ownership of Metromedia. The only commercial station locally owned today is controlled by the San Francisco Chronicle. But the basic point is simply that the national political power involved in ownership of a group of major VHF television stations in, say, New York, Los Angeles, Philadelphia, and

Washington, D.C., is greater than a democracy should unthinkingly repose in one man or corporation.

Conglomerate Corporations

For a variety of reasons, an increasing number of communications media are turning up on the organization charts of conglomerate companies. And the incredible profits generated by broadcast stations in the major markets (television broadcasters average a 90 to 100 percent return on tangible investment annually) have given FCC licensees, particularly owners of multiple television stations like the networks, Metromedia, Storer Broadcasting, and others, the extra capital with which to buy the New York Yankees (CBS), Random House (RCA), or Northeast Airlines (Storer). Established or up-and-coming conglomerates regard communications acquisitions as prestigious, profitable, and often a useful or even a necessary complement to present operations and projected exploitation of technological change.

The national problem of conglomerate ownership of communications media was well illustrated by the ITT-ABC case. But the conglomerate problem need not involve something as large as ITT-ABC or RCA-NBC. Among the national group owners of television stations are General Tire (RKO), Avco, Westinghouse, Rust Craft, Chris Craft, Kaiser, and Kerr-McGee. The problem of local conglomerates was forcefully posed for the FCC in another case earlier this year. Howard Hughes, through Hughes Tool Company, wanted to acquire one of Las Vegas' three major television stations. He had recently acquired $125 million worth of Las Vegas real estate, including hotels, gambling casinos, and an airport. These investments supplemented 27,000 acres previously acquired. The Commission majority blithely approved the television acquisition without a hearing, overlooking FCC precedents which suggested that a closer examination was in order. In each of these instances the potential threat is similar to that in the ITT-ABC case – that personal economic interests may dominate or bias otherwise independent media.

Concentration and Technological Change

The problem posed by conglomerate acquisitions of communications outlets is given a special but very important twist by the pendency of sweeping technological changes which have already begun to unsettle the structure of the industry.

President Johnson has appointed a distinguished task force to evaluate our national communications policy and chart a course for realization of these technological promises in a manner consistent with the public interest. But private interests have already begun to implement their own plans on how to deal with the revolution in communications technology.

General Sarnoff of RCA has hailed the appearance of "the knowledge industry" – corporate casserole dishes blending radio and television stations, networks, and programming; films, movie houses, and record companies; newspaper, magazine, and book publishing; advertising agencies; sports or other entertainment companies; and teaching machines and other profitable appurtenances of the $50 billion "education biz."

And everybody's in "cable television" – networks, book publishers, newspapers. Cable television is a system for building the best TV antenna in town and then wiring it into everybody's television set – for a fee. It improves signal quality and number of channels, and has proved popular. But the new technology is such that it has broadcasters and newspaper publishers worried. For the same cable that can bring off-the-air television into the home can also bring programming from the cable operator's studio, or an "electronic newspaper" printed in the home by a facsimile process. Books can be delivered (between libraries, or to the home) over "television" by using the station's signal during an invisible pause. So everybody's hedging their bets – including the telephone company. Indeed, about all the vested interests can agree upon is that none of them want us to have direct, satellite-to-home radio and television. But at this point it is not at all clear who will have his hand on the switch that controls what comes to the American people over their "telephone wire" a few years hence.

What is to be done?

It would be foolish to expect any extensive restructuring of the media in the United States, even if it were considered desirable. Technological change can bring change in structure, but it is as likely to be change to even greater concentration as to wider diversity. In the short run at least, economics seems to render essentially intractable such problems as local monopolies in daily newspapers, or the small number of outlets for national news through wire services, newsmagazines, and the television networks. Indeed, to a certain extent the very high technical quality of the performance rendered by these news-gathering organizations is aided by their concentration of resources into large units and the financial cushions of oligopoly profits.

Nevertheless, it seems clear to me that the risks of concentration are grave.

Chairman Philip Hart of the Senate Antitrust and Monopoly Subcommittee remarked by way of introduction to his antitrust subcommittee's recent hearings about the newspaper industry, "The products of newspapers, opinion and information, are essential to the kind of society that we undertake to make successful here." If we are serious about the kind of society we have undertaken, it is clear to me that we simply must not tolerate concentration of media ownership – except where concentration creates actual countervailing social benefits. These benefits cannot be merely speculative. They must be identifiable, demonstrable, and genuinely weighty enough to offset the dangers inherent in concentration.

This guideline is a simple prescription. The problem is to design and build machinery to fill it. And to keep the machinery from rusting and rotting. And to replace it when it becomes obsolete.

America does have available governmental machinery which is capable of scotching undue accumulations of power over the mass media, at least in theory and to some extent. The Department of Justice has authority under the antitrust laws to break up combinations which "restrain trade" or which "tend to lessen competition." These laws apply to the media as they do to any other industry.

But the antitrust laws simply do not get to where the problems are. They grant authority to block concentration only when it threatens economic competition in a particular economic market. Generally, in the case of the media, the relevant market is the market for advertising. Unfortunately, relatively vigorous advertising competition can be maintained in situations where competition in the marketplace of ideas is severely threatened. In such cases, the Justice Department has little inclination to act.

Look at the *Chicago Tribune*'s recent purchase of that city's most popular and most successful FM radio station. The *Tribune* already controlled two Chicago newspapers, one (clear channel) AM radio station, and the city's only independent VHF television station. It controls numerous broadcast, CATV, and newspaper interests outside Chicago (in terms of circulation, the nation's largest newspaper chain). But, after an investigation, the Antitrust Division let this combination go through. The new FM may be a needless addition to the *Tribune*'s already impressive battery of influential media; it could well produce an unsound level of concentration in the production and supply of what Chicagoans see, read, and hear about affairs in their community, in the nation, and in the world. But it did not threaten the level of competition for advertising money in any identifiable advertising market. So, it was felt, the acquisition was not the business of the Justice Department.

Only the FCC is directly empowered to keep media ownership patterns compatible with a democracy's need for diversified sources of opinion and information.

In earlier times, the Commission took this responsibility very seriously. In 1941, the FCC ordered NBC to divest itself of one of its two radio networks (which then became ABC), barring any single network from affiliating with more than one outlet in a given city. (The Commission has recently waived this prohibition for, ironically, ABC's four new national radio networks.) In 1941 the Commission also established its power to set absolute limits on the total number of broadcast licenses any individual may hold, and to limit the number of stations any individual can operate in a particular service area.

The American people are indebted to the much maligned FCC for establishing these rules. Imagine, for example, what the structure of political power in this country might look like if two or three companies owned substantially all of the broadcast media in our major cities.

But since the New Deal generation left the command posts of the FCC, this agency has lost much of its zeal for combating concentration. Atrophy has reached so advanced a state that the public has of late witnessed the bizarre spectacle of the Justice Department, with its relatively narrow mandate, intervening in FCC proceedings, such as ITT-ABC, to create court cases with names like *The United States vs. The FCC.*

This history is an unhappy one on the whole. It forces one to question whether government can ever realistically be expected to sustain a vigilant posture over an industry which controls the very access of government officials themselves to the electorate.

I fear that we have already reached the point in this country where the media, our greatest check on other accumulations of power, may themselves be beyond the reach of any other institution: the Congress, the President, or the Federal Communications Commission, not to mention governors, mayors, state legislators, and city councilmen. Congressional hearings are begun and then quietly dropped. Whenever the FCC stirs fitfully as if in wakefulness, the broadcasting industry scurries up the Hill for a congressional bludgeon. And the fact that roughly 60 percent of all campaign expenses go to radio and television time gives but a glimmer of the power of broadcasting in the lives of senators and congressmen.

However, the picture at this moment has its more hopeful aspect. There does seem to be an exceptional flurry of official concern. Even the FCC has its proposed rulemaking outstanding. The Department of Justice, having broken into the communications field via its dramatic intervention before the FCC in the ITT-ABC merger case, has also been pressing a campaign to force the dissolution of joint operating agreements between separately owned newspapers in individual cities, and opposed a recent application for broadcasting properties by newspaper interests in Beaumont, Texas. It has been scrutinizing cross-media combinations linking broadcasting, newspaper, and cable television outlets. On Capitol Hill, Senator Phil Hart's Antitrust and Monopoly Subcommittee and Chairman Harley Staggers' House Interstate and Foreign Commerce Committee have both summoned the Federal Communications Commission to appear before them in recent months, to acquaint the Commission with the committees' concern about FCC-approved increases in broadcast holdings by single individuals and companies, and about cross-ownership of newspapers, CATV systems, and broadcast stations. Representatives John Dingell, John Moss, and Richard Ottinger have introduced legislation which would proscribe network ownership of any nonbroadcast interests. And as I previously mentioned, President Johnson has appointed a task force to undertake a comprehensive review of national communications policy.

Twenty years ago Robert M. Hutchins, then chancellor of the University of Chicago, was named chairman of the "Commission on Freedom of the Press." It produced a thoughtful report, full of recommendations largely applicable today–including "the establishment of a new and independent [nongovernmental] agency to appraise and report annually upon the performance of the press," and urged "that the members of the press engage in vigorous mutual criticism." Its proposals are once again being dusted off and reread.

What is needed now, more than anything else, is to keep this flurry of interest alive, and to channel it toward constructive reforms. What this means, in practical fact, is that concern for media concentration must find an institutional home.

The Department of Justice has already illustrated the value of participation by an external institution in FCC decision-making. The developing concept of a special consumers' representative offers a potentially broader base for similar action.

But the proper place to lodge continuing responsibility for promoting diversity in the mass media is neither the FCC nor the Justice Department nor a congressional committee. The initiative must come from private sources. Plucky Nader-like crusaders such as John Banzhaf (who single-handedly induced the FCC to apply the "fairness" doctrine to cigarette commercials) have shown how responsive government can be to the skillful and vigorous efforts of even a lone individual. But there are more adequately staffed and funded private organizations which could play a more effective role in policy formation than a single individual. Even the FCC, where the public interest gets entirely too little representation from private sources, has felt the impact of the United Church of Christ, with its interest in the influence of broadcasting on race relations and in the programming responsibility of licensees, and of the American Civil Liberties Union, which submitted a brief in the ITT-ABC case.

Ideally, however, the resources for a sustained attack on concentration might be centered in a single institution, equipped to look after this cause with the kind of determination and intelligence that the Ford Foundation and the Carnegie Corporation, for example, have brought to bear in behalf of the cause of public broadcasting and domestic satellites. The law schools and their law reviews, as an institution, have performed well in this way for the courts, but have virtually abdicated responsibility for the agencies.

Such an organization could devote itself to research as well as representation. For at present any public body like the FCC, which has to make determinations about acceptable levels of media concentration, has to do so largely on the basis of hunch. In addition, private interest in problems of concentration would encourage the Justice Department to sustain its present vigilance in this area. It could stimulate renewed vigilance on the part of the FCC, through participation in Commission proceedings. And it could consider whether new legislation might be appropriate to reach the problem of newspaper-magazine-book publishing combinations.

If changes are to be made (or now dormant standards are to be enforced) the most pressing political question is whether to apply the standards prospectively only, or to require divestiture. It is highly unlikely, to say the least, that legislation requiring massive divestiture of multiple station ownership, or newspaper ownership of stations, would ever pass through Congress. Given the number of station sales every year, however, even prospective standards could have some impact over ten years or so.

In general, I would urge the minimal standard that no accumulation of media should be permitted without a specific and convincing showing of a continuing countervailing social benefit. For no one has a higher calling in an increasingly complex free society bent on self-government than he who informs and moves the people. Personal prejudice, ignorance, social pressure, and advertiser pressure are in large measure inevitable. But a nation that has, in Learned Hand's phrase, "staked its all" upon the rational dialogue of an informed electorate simply cannot take any unnecessary risk of polluting the stream of information and opinion that sustains it. At the very least, the burden of proving the social utility of doing otherwise should be upon him who seeks the power and profit which will result.

Whatever may be the outcome, the wave of renewed interest in the impact of ownership on the role of the media in our society is healthy. All will gain from intelligent inquiry by Congress, the Executive, the regulatory commissions – and especially the academic community, the American people generally, and the media themselves. For, as the Supreme Court has noted, nothing is more important in a free society than "the widest possible dissemination of information from diverse and antagonistic sources." And if we are unwilling to discuss this issue fully today we may find ourselves discussing none that matter very much tomorrow.

(b) Galloping Global Multi-Media Merger Mania:

A Former FCC Commissioner's Perspective

This portion of Chapter 7 comes from a text prepared for delivery to the Peoples Unitarian-Universalist Church, Cedar Rapids, Iowa, February 18, 2001.

Jefferson and Free Speech

Diversity is essential for political choice, for democratic choice. Not just a choice among political parties and candidates, but diversity in the sources of information that feed the minds of active citizens engaged in the radical experiment called self-governing.

Thomas Jefferson saw the modules of a democratic society as of a piece.

- *Public education* to provide the basic tools for receiving and thinking through information and arguments.
- *Public libraries* to make available to the poorest among us the stores of information available to kings.
- *Postal rates* for newspapers and books to encourage their circulation.
- *Free speech*, protected by a First Amendment, to encourage, and bolster the courage of, citizens contributing to a democratic dialogue in which there is no such thing as an illegal thought.
- *The right to vote*, to decide who our representatives shall be, who shall govern in our name. A right to vote that expanded from white, male, landowners over 21 to include over time all white males, African American males, females, and anyone over 18 years of age.

So how are we doing 200 years later?

As a school board member, I am as aware as anyone of the challenges confronting public education today. But I am also proud of our accomplishments. We get better than we deserve.

You have a great public library in Cedar Rapids. We've recently passed a bond issue to expand our award-winning public library in Iowa City. And both are responding to the challenge of a global Internet that can today bring into our homes intellectual and informational resources even beyond those of the Library of Congress.

It is the third module, the available diversity in the democratic dialogue, which most concerns me.

It is the subject about which you have asked me to speak.

Needless to say, those shortcomings are multiplied many times in our political campaigns, elections, and democratic governance.

Indeed, when fewer than 10 percent of us bother to vote for school board or city council members – and less than half for president – one can reasonably feel concern that we are no longer engaged in informed self-governing in this country.

An Overview

There are at least 11 points that need to be summarily touched upon. It is not a single phenomenon with which we are dealing. It is much worse, much more complicated, than that. Numerous undesirable trends are each re-enforcing each other.

- The relocation of the democratic dialogue from the conversations of ordinary citizens into the for-profit conduits of corporate media moguls.
- The repeal of the First Amendment for ordinary citizens.
- The increasing concentration of ownership of individual media, such as newspapers or television.
- The merger of different types of media into multi-media conglomerates.
- The growing global reach of these media conglomerates.
- Their corporate interlocks of directors, ownership and partnerships.
- The convergence of technologies.
- The impact of synergy on hype.
- The resulting creation of the superstar – and suppression of the merely talented.
- The multiplying of the range of incentives to corporate censorship.
- The erosion of journalism.

Who Speaks, and From Where

The first major change to note is where the information and dialogue are coming from.

I don't mean to disparage the importance of what we call "word-of-mouth." There are citizens' presentations such as this one, conversations over coffee in the cafes of rural Iowa, community meetings, posters on kiosks, machine-copied handouts, community video channels on cable, and individuals' Web sites and blogs. These are the remnants of Thomas Jefferson's notion of free speech.

But compare this flow of information and dialogue with the influence and quantity of that from, for example, *The New York Times*, *Wall Street Journal*, *Washington Post*, ABC, CBS, NBC, Fox and CNN. It is like comparing the flow from a garden hose to that of the Cedar River.

It is these multi-billion-dollar multiple-media conglomerates, with their global reach, that have the greatest influence in

- Young girls' acceptance of their own bodies
- Young boys attraction to violence as a technique of dispute resolution
- The willingness of blue-collar workers to accept an ever shrinking wage rather than join a labor union
- The audience's perception, from the media's choice of news, that events in the daily life of Paris Hilton equal in significance stories regarding the potential political consequences of global poverty, or the corporate corruption of the political process.

Nor is the forum, the place where the dialogue occurs, the only thing that has changed over time. So have the rules.

Repealing the First Amendment

What the Supreme Court did recently in choosing Bush over Gore by a five-to-four vote is as nothing compared to what they've done with the First Amendment.

Since the Court says the media's First Amendment right to speak includes its constitutional right to censor the speech of others, our only legally enforceable right to speak is conditioned on our finding the $100 million in spare pocket change that might enable us to buy our own newspaper or TV station.

Couple this with the ability of corporate employers to silence their workers, and we're left not with 300 million Americans, but something more like 10,000 who are still free meaningfully to exercise their First Amendment rights in a mass media society.

It is as if the Supreme Court decided to repeal the First Amendment and then not tell anyone about it.

Mergers, Deregulation and Convergence

Not only have we changed the forum, and given the gatekeepers of our media conduits the right to censor their content, there are some other unfortunate trends as well.

Media firms are getting larger and fewer. When Time and Warner merged, long before AOL was a relevant player, we asked them why. "Because some day," we were told, "there are going to be five firms controlling all the media on planet Earth and we intend to be one of them."

There are not yet five firms controlling all of the world's media. But that's clearly the trend. In music we're already there. Of all the music you hear on the radio, the CDs you buy, iTunes you download, the soundtracks of the movies you see, well over 95 percent of it is owned by five global firms.

The FCC, required by Congress to regulate media "in the public interest," used to have strict standards regarding ownership. Limits on how large a geographic area a station could reach. Limits on how many stations a single licensee could operate. Concerns about national media power. Regional media power. Joint ownership within a single market. Multiple media ownership.

No longer. "Deregulation" is the mantra of the day. Nor are the FTC or Antitrust Division of the Justice Department particularly concerned.

The media grab has been underway now for some time. So there are newspaper chains that own so-called "local" newspapers in dozens of cities. There are individual corporate licensees that operate as many as 1200 radio stations.

But that's the least of it.

Multiple-Media Conglomerates

The other thing that has been going on simultaneously is the creation of multiple media conglomerates. What I mean by that is a single company that not only has a dominant position in one medium, such as newspapers or radio stations, but in multiple media – book publishing, movie studios, magazines, broadcasting, videotape rentals, Internet service providers, and cable television.

Want an example? Let's use Time Warner – or, as it became, AOL Time Warner. At that time its Web site had pages called "Corporate Overview" and "Our Companies." They listed six *categories* of companies. Each category had within it what might be thought of as multiple corporate divisions. And those, in turn, contained companies.

AOL, for instance, was in fact 13 companies.

There were four network groups: Turner Entertainment, CNN, HBO and the WB TV Network. Turner Entertainment was 15 companies plus three joint ventures. CNN was 10 companies, 15 Web sites, and three joint ventures. HBO was 12 companies and 14 joint ventures. WB was two companies.

Publishing was represented by Time Inc. and Time Warner Trade. Time Inc. had 56 publications and what appeared to be 11 additional companies plus two joint ventures. Time Warner had five companies.

Filmed Entertainment included Warner Bros. and New Line Cinema. Warner had 15 companies, New Line had six.

Warner Music Group included 15 companies and 10 joint ventures.

Time Warner Cable didn't even bother to list all of the cable companies it owns, just the ones with more than 100,000 subscribers each. There were 35 of those. The Tampa Bay and New York City systems, for example, each had about 1 million subscribers. Time Warner Cable also owned 5 local news channels and had two additional joint ventures.

The other multiple media firms at that time were similar – News Corporation, Viacom, Disney, and AT&T.

Corporate Interlocks

As if this weren't bad enough, these firms are also buying into each other, going into joint ventures, and partnership agreements. As difficult as it is to know what any given company owns on any given day, it is even more difficult to know what other companies may, in effect, own a piece of it.

From time to time a publication called Multichannel News puts together a chart of these interlocking relationships. When I got out the 1999 version one day I didn't count all the boxes on the chart, but I would estimate there were at least 500. Initially I assumed that surely this chart must cover all of the various media companies involved.

But as I examined it more closely I realized that there were no book publishing subsidiaries listed. No magazines or newspapers. No movie studios. No broadcast stations. What this enormous, and enormously complex, chart reflects is only the interlocking relationships between the cable programming suppliers – a narrow slice of what the multi-media conglomerates control.

Convergence

And while this has been happening the digital transformation has enabled a technological convergence.

What do I mean by "convergence"? Want some practical illustrations?

You can get streaming audio and video on your computer screen from radio stations and TV program providers, and get access to the World Wide Web on your television set.

It is becoming increasingly difficult to tell one electronic pocket device from another. You can send e-mail from a pager, use your cell phone to surf the Internet, and your pocket computer to take digital photographs.

Convergence is well illustrated in the single desktop device that can perform as a telephone, fax machine, copier, scanner and printer – all in one box.

So what used to be a telephone company can now deliver a cable television service. The former cable company wants to be my Internet service provider. And my present Internet service provider gives me access from my computer to a free long distance telephone company – as well as a free "voicemail" service when I'm getting access to the Internet over a conventional phone line.

In other words, there's a kind of technological imperative driving at least some of this multiple media merging.

Synergy: Hype and Superstars

The consequence is a radical alteration in the content, and the marketing, of media. The owners call it "synergy." In generating profits the whole becomes a multiple of the parts.

So what? Consider this scenario:

A multiple media conglomerate's book-publishing subsidiary gives a $5 million book advance to a popular author. The book is reviewed, excerpted and heavily advertised, in magazines and newspapers owned by the conglomerate. It's promoted in bookstores owned by the conglomerate. The author appears on talk shows on the radio and television stations and networks owned by the conglomerate. Successful marketing makes it a best seller.

So much so that one of the movie studios owned by the conglomerate contracts with the author, and a screenwriter, to begin the process of making a feature film – a possibility envisioned before the book was even written. The film is advertised on television networks owned by the conglomerate, the stars are interviewed on their late night talk shows, and the film is shown in their movie theaters.

After the theater run the film is shown on their television networks, and then distributed to the cable systems it owns from the cable program supplier it owns by way of the communications satellite it either owns or leases.

Finally, it is made available for videotape or DVD sale and rental through their chain of video rental stores.

And while all of this is going on in this country, the process is being duplicated around the world through the conglomerate's foreign subsidiaries. In fact, media is one of our nation's more successful exports in terms of balance of payments.

So what's wrong with this? There are at least a couple of things.

These ownership patterns have a corrupting influence throughout all media.

How can a book reviewer, or late night talk show producer or interviewer, maintain the independence and integrity we, the audience, assume and rely upon? There is enormous pressure for what we used to think of as independent evaluation and criticism to become little more than a contribution to a marketing effort, or hype. This takes the form of both what products are chosen for any comment at all, as well as what is said about them.

Because so much money is riding on an individual book or movie there is much less room for risk. Gone are the days when a dedicated book or newspaper publisher might decide to publish a worthy first novel, or pursue an important bit of investigative journalism, knowing the projects would inevitably produce a financial loss.

And re-enforcing those pressures is the drive to create the superstar.

Global superstar status is why a Michael Jordan could earn more from Nike for endorsing their products than Nike pays to all their Southeast Asian workers combined for manufacturing them. Corporations manufacture celebrities in music, drama and sports because it's an easier and a more profitable form of marketing than limiting the focus to talent and content.

As a result of the gross disparities in pay between the superstar and those who are merely extraordinarily gifted the owners need to radically reduce the number of people at the bottom of the ladder in order to pay the one person at the top.

Thus, what we lose from this marketing, as an audience and a society, is the richness and variety of entertainment, information and culture now denied us. The more that we, too, want to see and hear the superstars of sports, TV, music and movies, the less we see of the equally, or more, talented in our midst. The less is the incentive for a young person to become a starving actor, and join that 80 percent of the Screen Actors Guild membership that earns less than $3000 a year from their craft.

Corporate Content Censorship

Who among us is anxious to tell the world about the things we have done of which we are most ashamed?

It's only natural that corporations also want to put their best foot forward.

Why would a TV network want its news division to do a series about how network executives order writers to insert more violence into episodic television scripts than the writers think appropriate?

Why would the *Wall Street Journal* want to do a piece revealing the percentage of their daily content that comes directly from the public relations releases of major corporations?

They wouldn't.

We might hope for more. But so long as owners and journalists are human asking them to be self-critical is really expecting too much.

But if newspapers are willing to be critical of television, and broadcasters are willing to lobby against the interests of cable systems, and telephone companies take no interest in content at all, we can live with the consequences.

The problem arises when, for example, a major nuclear power plant manufacturer, such as GE, acquires NBC News. Or when Disney acquires ABC. The result is to substantially reduce, if not silence entirely, NBC's candid appraisal of the risks of nuclear power plants, and ABC's willingness to report on Disney's hiring pedophiles. (The experience of ABC's investigative reporter Brian Ross regarding the latter is discussed in the book by Peter and Rochelle Schweizer, *Disney: The Mouse Betrayed*.)

When I was an FCC Commissioner, and ITT wanted to acquire ABC, ITT's CEO, Harold Geneen, told me that he had over 400 boards of directors reporting to him. When conglomerates reach that size, and diversity, corporate censorship begins to cover a dangerously wide range of subjects.

We are living in an age when, as the former CBS News President Fred Friendly was fond of putting it, "what you don't know can kill you." Not only is that true in the literal sense, it is also true in the figurative sense of the death of the democratic dialogue essential to self-governing.

Where Have All the Journalists Gone?

What sometimes appears from an historic distance to be a golden age often turns out, upon closer examination, to be little more than yellow journalism.

It is certainly true that the media business has always been a business. Early 20th Century newspaper publishers were as interested in increasing circulation and advertising revenues as their counterparts are today.

Although, in fairness to them, it should be noted in passing that Joseph Pulitzer put his one principle on the masthead: "to make it harder for the rich to grow richer and easier for the poor to keep from growing poorer." William Randolph Hearst wrote, "This newspaper hopes for a labor union victory and means to help it along because the public welfare demands it." When was the last time you heard sentiments like that from one of today's media moguls?

One could argue that the Internet provides more free access to journalism – albeit larded with advertising – than was ever available in the past.

But A. J. Liebling's observation is still accurate as well. He pointed out that the first thing to go, following the loss of competition among taverns, was the free lunch. Similarly, he said, news is the first thing to go following the loss of competition among newspapers.

Just as we have substituted junk food for the blue plate special, so have we substituted junk news for traditional journalism. It's what Walter Lippmann once characterized in the book *Public Opinion* as "side shows and three-legged calves."

What Paddy Cheyefsky predicted in the 1976 movie, "Network," has not only come to our TV screens but has actually become worse. A TV critic once observed of entertainment television, "It is impossible to write anything of social consequence for a show like 'Gomer Pyle.'" Sadly, it is becoming increasingly difficult to present anything of social consequence on television's talk and panel programs as well – let alone to do so with civility.

Nor is local TV news much better. All too often fender-bender accidents, fires, high school sports, commercials and weather – do we really need to know the precise temperature in every Iowa town? – drive out the local stories we really do need to know.

But it is not just pandering and ratings. It's also costs and profits.

The "Extreme Football League" (XFL) – "extreme" as in "extremely bad taste" – costs NBC a lot less to produce than the NFL games. The fantasy called "reality television" – such as "Temptation Island" – costs a lot less than paying skilled writers and professional actors.

And so it is with journalism. A lot of television news is created by folks who read *The New York Times* in the morning, take pictures of those stories in the afternoon, and put them on the air in the evening. News bureaus, especially those outside the U.S., cost a lot of money to create and maintain. Abolish a bureau and the cost savings fall all the way to the bottom line where they are immediately transformed into profits.

Jingoism in the Global Village

The problem with this kind of "downsizing," of course, is that you end up with someone in a Paris news bureau who suddenly discovers she is now responsible for covering the whole of Africa as well.

In 2001 you may have heard something about the election in Israel and the earthquake in India.

But ask yourself, how much did you then know of the relevance of the snowfall in Afghanistan – or what was then going on along its border with Pakistan? The big story out of Myanmar? The Congo? Indonesia? Sri Lanka?

This is supposed to be the age of the global village, international economic competition, Friedman's *The World is Flat*. We fear terrorists we've never heard of, and have a constantly eroding balance of payments.

And yet, if it weren't for WSUI's carriage of the BBC's World Service I'd have a tough time finding out what is going on outside the limited, jingoistic focus of America's media.

Conclusion

I would like to end on a more optimistic note, but I don't have the tonal range I once did.

So I will close by merely repeating the themes we've briefly touched upon:

- The relocation of the democratic dialogue from the conversations of ordinary citizens into the for-profit conduits of corporate media moguls.
- The repeal of the First Amendment for ordinary citizens.
- The increasing concentration of ownership of individual media, such as newspapers or television.
- The merger of different types of media into multi-media conglomerates.
- The growing global reach of these media conglomerates.
- Their corporate interlocks of directors, ownership and partnerships.
- The convergence of technologies and industries.
- The impact of synergy on hype.
- The resulting creation of the superstar – and suppression of the merely talented.
- The multiplying of the range of incentives to corporate censorship.
- The erosion of journalism.

Each is, alas, a subject you are not likely to hear much about on the evening news.

Chapter Eight: Global Media

Georgia's Media Future: A Personal View of Options and Opportunities

Chapter 8 is drawn from a paper that grew out of the author's consultations in the Republic of Georgia February 24-March 3, 1998, and the material prepared prior to, and following, that trip. An early version was written March 12, 1998. Another version was published as "Georgia's Media Future: Options and Opportunities for the Third Millennium" in Laura Lengel, ed., Culture @nd Technology in the New Europe: Civic Discourse in Transformation in Post-Communist Nations (Stamford: Ablex Publishing 2000), Chapter 17, pp. 323-37.

Introduction

The ideas, discussion, and proposals which follow are not only "not necessarily the views of ABA/CEELI, the Federal Communications Commission or other U.S. Government agencies, the University of Iowa, or other institutions with which I am or have been affiliated."

In this case, much of this paper is known by me to express views directly contrary to the views of those institutions – to the extent that they have positions on these issues at all.

Having spent much of my seven-year career as an FCC commissioner writing dissenting opinions in matters resolved by votes of six to one, that doesn't bother me. As someone has observed before me, "Every new idea is, at its inception, supported by a minority of one."

But I would not want to leave any ambiguity regarding the support of others for these ideas.

This paper is not my comments on the legislation currently under consideration in Georgia. Those comments are contained in a separate document.

This is simply the expression of some personal views.

So why do I bother to write this at all?

My work on behalf of the Georgia Parliament is as a volunteer. Even though I am unpaid, I take that work, and that relationship, seriously.

It is not my role to try to create future legal business as a "rainmaker" for a law firm. (Indeed, I am not practicing law.)

I am not trying to create future business for any American industry or individual corporation. (I deliberately do not have such affiliations.)

I did not go to Georgia to push any organization's ideological agenda.

I believe such roles would be inappropriate, even where I so inclined.

I am happy to have been asked to participate in the ABA/CEELI-Georgia Parliament effort to review proposed legislative language, section by section, line by line – most recently during a visit to Tbilisi, Georgia, from February 24 through March 3, 1998. That is important work. I have done some of it, and will do more – elsewhere than in this document.

The story is told of the three bricklayers who were asked what they were doing. "I'm carrying bricks," said one. "I'm making a wall," said the second. "I'm building a cathedral," said the third.

Media and telecommunications policy are central to the functioning of any society. They affect – among other things – economic growth, the education of the young, levels of democratic participation, the preservation of the culture, and the values of the people about everything from the role of women to the role of war – essentially every aspect of being human and living in a civilized community.

So I'm happy to carry the bricks and build the wall, but I would also like to offer my view from the top of the cathedral.

Most of these ideas will be (or have been) rejected by Georgians as they have been by North Americans. So I will be neither surprised nor disappointed if this paper has little or no effect on Georgia's future.

But I believe it would be irresponsible of me not to at least offer these ideas for consideration.

World Class Electronic Media for Georgia's Future: Some Alternatives

With rare exception, the assumption underlying most of the papers I have seen, and discussions in which I participated, is that Georgia should attempt to construct a broadcasting system, using analog technology, similar to that in the U.S. in the 1960s and 1970s: a public broadcasting system relatively independent of the government (to replace "State Television"), along with commercial television stations licensed and regulated by an independent body similar to the U.S. Federal Communications Commission.

That is one option. It appears to be the option on its way to adoption. There are, however, alternative options.

The following idea, or approach, was discussed with very few individuals, and none who responded to it positively. The response was not negative; the focus was simply on other issues and approaches. It is included here anyway because (a) I truly do believe it is worth serious consideration by Georgians, and (b) it may be found of interest in the future by individuals with whom I did not have the opportunity to discuss it during my recent visit.

There are disadvantages to building a telecommunications and broadcasting system "from scratch," from the ground up. There may be a shortage of capital, and experienced personnel. There may be an absence of audience expectation. In the case of Georgia, there is also the pre-existing state broadcasting system to overcome.

But there are also advantages.

One of the advantages is the opportunity to "leapfrog" intermediate technologies. It is not necessary to create the analog broadcasting system of the 1960s in order to evolve toward the 21st Century. One can start with a 21st Century digital system and simply skip the technologies of the 1960s, 1970s, 1980s and 1990s.

There are also disadvantages to creating a 1960s television system.

(a) TV stations are costly: studios, transmitters, antenna towers, cameras, and so forth.

(b) Homeowners' total investment in receivers is a multiple of the station owners' costs.

(c) Nor do these costs produce much in the way of benefits. Unless an even more costly nationwide repeater/translator transmitter/antenna system is installed, vast areas of the country will be without any TV reception.

(d) And one of the consequences of an over-the-air technology is the creation of an artificial limitation on the number and diversity of channels, with the resulting concentration of economic, political and media power in the hands of a very few.

I do not know enough about either (a) the Georgian economy, society and technological capability, or (b) the characteristics and costs of available technology, to make precise recommendations.

But this portion of this paper is not about precise recommendations anyway. It's about a "new paradigm," a new way of thinking about Georgia's telecommunications and media future. So the ideas that follow are merely examples designed to stimulate discussion, suggestive illustrations of the type of options that may be available to those who are planning, and building, Georgia's future. Those who are open to new paradigm ways of thinking will almost certainly come up with approaches that are not mentioned here, are far better, and certainly better suited to Georgia.

(1) **Satellite broadcasting**. Small (50 cm) dishes for reception of satellite signals (with the accompanying receivers and other equipment) are now relatively cheap. Presumably, with the research and development, science and engineering capability in Georgia, they could be built in-country (thereby providing jobs and otherwise improving the economy). The satellite uplink, and the satellite itself, are, of course, more expensive. Perhaps satellite channels could be

leased, rather than owning the satellite. Perhaps foundations or other aid-granting institutions, or even corporations, could be interested in contributing funding.

Investigation may show that such a system would not be more expensive than the cost of providing a country-wide coverage of Georgia using conventional, over-the-air broadcasting technology. Even if it were to be slightly more expensive, among the advantages of such a system are that:

(a)   it provides full-country coverage throughout Georgia,

(b)   100-500 channels can provide outlets for substantially more "broadcasters" than an over-the-air system,

(c)   it can also be used for Internet (data) communication (at least one-way, from the source to the user),

(d)   unlike cable and "telephone" video delivery systems the incremental cost of adding an additional home viewer is virtually zero,

(e)   it avoids the cost, aesthetic blight, and other difficulties associated with "wiring up" every home in Georgia, and

(f)   of course, it also avoids the costs associated with transmitters, antenna towers, translators, and the other capital costs of establishing conventional over-the-air stations.

(2) Cable television. Cable television is only 10 or 20 years newer than over-the-air technology. It is usually installed "over" (*i.e.*, after, in addition to) a broadcasting system, providing an alternative way of distributing programming from TV stations (through a wire, rather than through the air).

Of course, it is also possible for a cable system to create its own programming, or contract with programming suppliers (who often use satellites to distribute their product). Although there is no theoretical limit to the number of channels a cable system can provide (by stringing additional cables) many U.S. cable companies offer only 35 channels. Unless required to do otherwise, the cable company, normally a monopoly, will seek to profit maximize by charging as much as possible for as little programming as possible – while maintaining a non-reviewable control, or censorship, over all channels.

Note that, rather than using a cable system as an alternative distribution network for over-the-air stations' signals, it could be created as the sole method for bringing audio and video programming into Georgians' homes. Presumably, such a system would need to be created as a "common carrier;" that is, a system that would be forbidden to have any interest in the programming, and would be required to add such additional channels as are necessary to satisfy programmers' demand – at fair, regulated, equal prices for all.

(3) Video dialtone. An alternative to "cable television" would be to create a "telephone" system capable of handling voice, data, fax, and video. Cable television typically has no capacity for switching – a basic necessity for conventional telephone systems. The video dialtone option would be otherwise similar to that for cable television: a common carrier.

(4) Internet. The distribution of video signals is now in its infancy on the Internet. But, then, so were photos and audio not that many years ago. Today the video pictures are small, sometimes jerky, and the quality is not that good. But there are now plans to expand the capacity of the Internet by 100 times, or even 1000 times.

Many radio stations now "broadcast" their signal over the Internet simultaneously with conventional broadcast over the air. Presumably the day will soon come when this will be true for TV stations as well.

Georgia could (perhaps) take the plunge, with a ten year plan, say, for conversion to Internet distribution of what is today thought of as "television" programming. Because "telephone" conversations are now possible over the Internet, and fax transmissions, Georgia could find itself the world leader in this field.

(5) Wireless Internet. Of course, one of the drawbacks to Internet alternatives in Georgia today is that connection to the Internet is normally made with a "modem" through conventional telephone lines – which are both slow and not always reliable for this purpose. There is also the problem of electric power outages, but presumably these would be resolved by the time the Internet conversion was in place.

The discussion of satellite distribution, above, refers to "downloading" Internet material to a small dish. Such a system would still require uploading – today through the telephone system. However, it is also possible to provide wireless connections between an Internet Service Provider and a user. Not only does this avoid the problems (and costs) associated with telephone wire connections, it also substantially increases the possible speeds of transmission.

As explained at the beginning of this section, I am not recommending any of these ideas – and certainly not all of them. What I am recommending is that they be used as a stimulus for "what if" games, for thinking about (and then planning and building) possible future telecommunications and media systems.

I would like to see Georgia use the new communications technologies that are now available and can better position the country to provide education for its children, jobs for its adults, and a better quality of life and more democratic society for all.

Democratizing the Media: Some Alternatives

In America it has been said, "freedom of the press exists for the person who owns one." Of course, anyone can speak in the public park, or hand out leaflets on the public sidewalks. But the only citizens with meaningful First Amendment rights are those who have the capital, and the inclination, to acquire a major newspaper or broadcasting station.

Needless to say, virtually all media owners support this view.

Less expected, perhaps, is that the Supreme Court of the United States does also. The Court says that the "freedom of speech" includes the freedom not to speak; or, more precisely, the right to keep others from speaking. The Court has ruled that media owners can censor the views of those who would like to engage in a community's democratic dialogue by using the pages of its newspapers, or time on its radio and television stations. The point is that, not only do citizens not have the right to free newspaper space and broadcast time, they do not even have the right to buy space or time if the owner wishes to silence their viewpoint.

Thus, the position that follows is my own. It is not the view of most lawyers, judges, law or journalism professors – nor is it the view of some of the professional journalists with whom I spoke in Georgia (though they are quite insistent that they should have free speech rights vis-a-vis their employer-owners).

I believe that a democracy requires that all citizens have the potential right to participate in the democratic dialogue in a meaningful way (whether they choose to exercise that right or not).

A media owner should have the right to operate a newspaper or broadcast station with no advertising (for example, with support from subscribers, contributors, foundations, or from the owner's personal wealth). But if an owner does choose to sell space or time I believe he or she should not have the right to sell to some and not others. Especially is this true if there are a limited number of outlets reaching most of the community (as is true in all but the very largest cities).

Of course, I do not advocate that *all* advocacy ads need be taken, only that the reasonable and rational selection process not be based on content.

Whatever one's position on this issue, there are other possible ways of democratizing and diversifying the media that are far less controversial – and well within American law. Many of these options did seem to be of interest, and potentially acceptable, to the Georgians with whom I spoke. That is, there was a willingness to consider alternatives to a top down, hierarchal control of all content by a single media owner (whether state, public or corporate).

(1) Producer power. Within the contemplated "public broadcasting" alternative to state broadcasting there seemed to be support for the idea that the administrative budget and staff be kept lean, and that funding should go directly to producers (rather than through administrators). Indeed, a form of competition for these funds was proposed by some Georgians. Such an approach will encourage greater diversity as well as creativity.

(2) Political and reply time. There seemed to be support for a number of proposals growing out of the American experience with "equal opportunity" (the Section 315 requirement that if a station puts on one candidate for public office it is required to give an equal opportunity to all competitors), and the F.C.C.'s "personal attack doctrine," providing that citizens may be attacked by broadcast media owners, but that the attack triggers a right in the person attacked to know what was said and to reply personally.

There was a belief that at least public, and possibly commercial broadcasting as well, should make free time available to candidates. The idea was most recently proposed in the U.S. as a partial payback by broadcasters for the $70 billion worth frequencies given them by Congress and the F.C.C., for free, for high definition television.

The "fairness doctrine," found in part in Section 315 of the Communications Act, required that licenses must cover "controversial issues of public importance" and, in doing so, must present a range of views. It was only touched upon briefly, but there was little or no rejection of that idea (although the F.C.C. had repealed the doctrine).

(3) Community access cable channels. In the U.S. cable companies are required to make some of their channels available, for free, to designated institutions (such as local government, or public schools) and also to individual citizens. Without detailing either the history or specific requirements, such programming is, for the most part, not subject to cable company censorship. Thus, any citizen with access to a video camera can present his or her views to the community. There seemed to be some openness to this concept in Georgia as well.

(4) Access is fairness. Although never adopted by the F.C.C., when the fairness doctrine was under attack there was a proposal that radio and television stations wishing to opt out of its requirements could do so by offering a fixed percentage of each segment of their broadcast day for the purpose of (usually one-minute) announcements by local community groups. Of course, not all tendered announcements would have to be broadcast, but the system of selection would have to be other than content based.

(5) Ownership limitations. All Georgians (to the best of my recollection) were agreed that there should be some limitations on the numbers of stations any one owner can control. There was no objection to my proposal that this limit be set at one station per licensee. Whatever the statutory limitation ends up being, obviously the more owners there are the greater is the potential diversity of programming and opinion.

(6) Shared time stations. Giving every station licensee the right to broadcast 24 hours a day, seven days a week, creates an artificial limit on the number of "broadcasters" and the diversity of their programming. An obvious solution is "shared time." Under this approach everyone who wants to broadcast can do so. For example, if there are ten persons who wish to broadcast and only five stations, each can broadcast (a) a half-day, everyday, or (b) a whole day, three or four days a week. As more wish to broadcast there is less time per day for each; as some go out of business there is more time to share. Administrative arrangements would be made to fairly share the costs of construction, and operation, of the stations.

(7) Citizens media reform organizations. There is at this point little Georgian experience with the voluntary organizations so familiar in the U.S. from the time of de Tocqueville to the present. Media reform organizations in particular have played a very significant role in the U.S. in encouraging greater F.C.C. scrutiny of stations' performance, the creation of standards (and legislation) regarding children's' programming, or the reduction in levels of violence in television programs.

(8) Ombudspersons, letters and news councils. How can the public participate in the process of mass media selection and distribution of news? Some U.S. newspapers have in-house "ombudspersons" (a Scandinavian concept and word), independent of management and journalists, to receive – and respond publicly, in the paper – to complaints from the public. Some papers – and even radio and television programs – receive, and read, letters from the public critical of the programming. News councils are independent bodies of citizens – normally with no legal power – that hear, and write opinions regarding, public complaints about the media.

(9) Media literacy. TV viewers in most countries, and especially those brought up on state television, accept TV programming as a given, something they are powerless (and disinclined) to affect. TV advertising is most effective with viewers who are relatively unsophisticated about the way commercials are created, and the techniques used to manipulate consumer choice. By including media literacy courses throughout the K-12 school system it is possible to create a much more sophisticated television audience. Viewers can become more willing to make their own programs, to organize and present their views to stations and regulators, and to be more resistant to commercial appeals.

The point is that, just as there are options offered by new technology, so are there options with regard to the degree of direct citizen participation in the democratic dialogue. It is my impression that Georgians are interested in including many of these in their broadcasting practices, policy and law.

The Pros and Cons of Television

These thoughts are deliberately left to last because they will be considered by many to be among the most radical, or crazy, of those presented in this paper.

Even so, I believe it better to consider and reject them than to fail to consider them at all.

The advantages to a country of having a television system in place are well known.

Clearly, TV is very popular with viewers everywhere.

In the U.S. the average American watches TV four hours a day; the average set is turned on seven hours a day.

The marketplace indicates that consumers everywhere are willing to make financial sacrifices, to forego other purchases, to have a TV.

In the U.S., where the multiple-channel offerings of cable are widely available, roughly 70% of all home dwellers are willing – not only to buy a TV receiver – but to pay $15 to $50 a month for the cable service.

Television has proven itself to be one of the most powerful of all advertising media for the creation, and manipulation, of consumer demand. It can be a powerful engine driving a consumer economy – if that is something desired as a matter of national policy.

When the whole nation turns to television – such as in times of national disaster, or national joy – TV can be both a useful means of communication and of unification.

Television can be used to divert and defuse what might otherwise be citizen protests, or government opposition. It is the "electronic circus" in the modern version of governing through "bread and circuses."

Once in place, of course, it is politically somewhere between exceedingly difficult and impossible to radically alter, let alone to do away with, television.

Nonetheless, the disadvantages of television should be considered.

Many argue that it is harmful for children under the age of eight to be exposed to any television – regardless of content. (See, *e.g.*, Marie Winn, *The Plug-in Drug* (New York: Viking, 1977).) The argument is that young children have a lot of learning to do; that many end up watching television for as many as 50 hours a week; and that the act of watching television – sitting motionless, "relating" to an electronic device – impedes their growth physically, emotionally, intellectually, socially, and spiritually.

As children grow older, there appears to be an inverse relationship between the amount of time spent watching television and their academic achievement; the more they watch the lower their grades in school.

There are now over 2000 studies documenting the relationship between children's watching of televised violence and the amount of real-life violence in their behavior; some studies indicate the correlation is between the amount of time spent watching *any* television and violence, not just violent TV programs.

There is an opportunity cost associated with adults' TV watching; time spent watching TV is time unavailable for other activities: physical exercise, interaction with one's children, adult education. Among the first activities to go are the evening meetings necessary to a civic society and its organizations – including democratic political activity.

To the extent the television is commercial TV, the consequences change radically. Commercial TV is not about programs; it is about delivering the audience ("the product"), to the advertiser ("the consumer") at a cost-per-thousand viewers. Of all the objectionable "lowest common denominator" programming it will be the "least objectionable program" ("LOP;" commercial broadcasting's expression, not mine) that will command the largest audience (and, therefore, profit for the broadcaster).

Not only does commercial broadcasting have an incentive to use cheap-to-produce programming that gets the audience's attention through violence, chase scenes, crime, and sexual themes. In doing so, it tends to drive out the teaching, and values, of parents, churches, schools and the dominant culture. In their place it substitutes the values of materialism, hedonism, consumerism, conspicuous consumption – the notion that "you will be known by the companies you keep," that your identity comes from the brands you use.

As a consequence of television's dominance in the economy, and the lives of the citizens, the station owners soon take on a disproportionate political influence as well. For example, I was told that it is already the case in Georgia that the Parliament was reluctant to impose as strict a prohibition on the TV advertising of tobacco and alcohol as it might have because of the political power of the broadcasters.

There are many reasons why a nation might wish to create, or expand, its television system. There are other reasons why, even if it does not wish to do so, it must do so anyway because of political pressure.

But there are other reasons why it might wish to curtail the growth of television – or at least minimize its adverse consequences. One of the options would be an alternative medium: radio.

Radio in Lieu of Television

One of the central problems confronting Georgia in creating a broadcasting system is lack of resources.

Until the economy substantially improves there cannot be a lot of disposable income, and demand for consumer goods. Without the existence of such a market there is little reason to advertise. Without advertising, there is little income for commercial television. And without the prospect of commercial television income there is little incentive for investors to make a capital investment in stations.

Nor are the economic prospects for "public television" much better. Viewers have little interest in, or experience with, special taxes for television. They believe they have a right to television programming for free. Needless to say, there is even less tradition of voluntary contributions (such as U.S. public television relies upon for support). To the extent public television sells commercials, and becomes dependent on corporate advertisers, it enters into the same ratings game as, and becomes almost indistinguishable from, commercial television. Finally, the more public television is dependent upon the state for financing the more difficult it will be to project an image, and reality, of an independent public television system (as distinguished from the traditional state controlled television).

Given the economic realities confronting Georgia at this time, a two-phase plan might be worth consideration. The first phase would involve the development of a national public radio system. A two or three channel system, with nationwide coverage, could be developed for roughly one-tenth of what a national television system would cost.

Once this system was in place, the audience had become accustomed to "public broadcasting," the staff was assembled, the programming developed, the financial support firm and adequate – all at a fraction of the cost of television – the second phase could begin. The second phase would be public television.

Radio has advantages over television in addition to the cost savings in transmission.

Georgia has (at least at the present time) an electric power system that involves power outages during significant periods of time. It is much more common (as well as cheaper) for the audience to have alternative power systems for radio receivers than for television: batteries, solar power, or internal power generators (a "dynamo").

There are significantly more channels (frequencies) available for radio broadcasting in the AM and FM bands than TV channels. Thus, radio offers the opportunity for a greater democratization of the broadcast media, more diversity, than TV. This distinction is multiplied by the fact that it is much cheaper for a potential broadcaster to go into the radio business, rather than television.

It is cheaper – both for the broadcaster, and the audience – to provide nationwide radio coverage than television signals of similar reach. Radio signals can go farther, on less power, than TV. At night, AM radio can cover enormous distances. And, for the reasons mentioned above, radio receivers (which cost less than TVs) can be used anywhere in the country – with or without electric power facilities.

There are those who would argue that radio programming does less harm than TV programming. It leaves more intellectual and artistic freedom to the audience member – who must make his or her own pictures inside their head.

Of all the ideas I put forward, the proposal that public radio be given priority attention is the one that received the least interest – primarily because of the inevitability of a television system once the people have become dependent upon it. I nonetheless believe it is worthwhile passing along. Others may find it of greater appeal. Or there may be elements of, or variations on, the idea that may prove practical.

Conclusion

These are exciting times for Georgia. A nation with a great cultural heritage, a nation that has survived centuries of challenge, is entering a new era. Dangers and challenges abound – but so do opportunities and options.

Central to Georgia's future, in my view, will be the decisions regarding its public policy and laws affecting media and telecommunications. Those decisions will be made by Georgians; they must be made by Georgians.

That Georgia's leadership is open to new ideas, to alternatives to its past as it plans for its future, is one of the many strengths of this country and its people.

This paper represents but one U.S. citizen's effort to contribute to that process – with appreciation for the invitation to participate, and confidence in the ultimate result.

PART THREE: What Lies Ahead

Chapter Nine: Regulating the Internet

(a) Media Regulation in the Age of the Internet

This portion of Chapter 9 is drawn from some of the notes for a campus-wide lecture delivered while serving as the University of California Regents' Professor at the University of California San Diego. It was presented in the UCSD Copley Auditorium, February 1, 2000.

Overview

Talking about media, regulation or the Internet these days reminds me of that story about Albert Einstein. "Professor Einstein," a concerned student told him after being handed the exam, "these are the same questions as on last year's exam." Einstein replied, "Ah, yes, young man, the questions are the same, but all the answers have changed."

Here are some of the questions for which our answers seem to be changing as well:

1. What do we mean by "media" in an information environment that includes list servs and Matt Drudge?

2. What do we mean by "regulation" of a place called "cyberspace" that is both everywhere and nowhere at the same time?

3. And what on earth do we mean by "the Internet" – after we come to realize that it is not, after all, on earth?

4. Have bits and bytes eaten up whatever was left of what we used to call "copyright"?

5. We used to say, in a pre-feminist era, "Ours is a government of laws and not of men." A Yale law professor turned this on its head with, "Ours is a government of lawyers and not of men." To what

extent, when it comes to Internet regulation, do we need to revise it once again to "Ours is a government of engineers and not of lawyers." That is, to what extent is the regulation of the Internet – deliberately or inadvertently – the result of the designed-in architecture of the technology?

6. And what of the First Amendment? It was written at a time when the technology and economics of newspapers were far different from today. No one had even dreamed of radio and television – let alone the Internet. Do its words mean anything today – literally, figuratively or in spirit?

7. Convergence. How can we even begin to think about regulating a thing that is looking more and more like a big wad of chewing gum?

Those are not our only questions, but they're a place to start.

Media

If the Internet is not media somebody better tell the old, conventional 1960s giants that are still among us – the commercial TV networks, television and radio stations, the leading national newspapers and magazines – because they've all gone "dot.com"

Who's a "journalist" these days? If the *National Enquirer* can have its protected place on the newsstand along with the *Los Angeles Times*, by what rationale should Matt Drudge be entitled to fewer privileges and protections just because his "journalism" exists only in electronic form? There are many list servs that distribute their participants' comments to far more subscribers than can be claimed by many hard copy print publications. There are audio streaming services on the Internet with more listeners than many licensed radio stations.

So, yes, I think we have to treat the Internet as "media."

Regulation

There are some ways in which the regulation of media is no different from any other business: Zoning regulations control where they can build antenna towers. OSHA requirements apply to media workers' safety. The NLRB enforces their rights to unionize. They must fill out IRS tax forms like all the rest of us, and comply with the SEC's requirements when they sell stock.

So when we talk about regulation of media we are usually talking about:

1. Licensing requirements

2. Ownership limitations

3. Prohibitions on speech, such as obscenity, fraud or defamation

4. Required speech, such as former FCC requirements for local news

5. Access requirements, such as the public access channels on cable, or the equal opportunity requirements for broadcasters during campaigns

Bear in mind that at the time of broadcasting's beginnings virtually every nation on earth simply assumed that the technology's potential power and influence were such that it could not be trusted to private hands. In some countries that meant ownership and operation by the government. In others it meant a public corporation – a distinction seldom grasped by either broadcasters or regulators in this country.

"Regulation" presumes some measure of private participation. It also recognizes an unwillingness to leave that private participation entirely to the forces of the marketplace.

Beginning in the 1970s, accelerating in the 1980s, and continuing to this day has been the mantra of "marketplace regulation" or "deregulation."

Obviously, I do not favor regulation for its own sake – for any industry. If a relatively unregulated market does an adequate job of providing innovation, consumer safety, choice and competitive pricing I see no reason to regulate it. Examples in my home town of Iowa City, Iowa, probably would include clothing and grocery stores.

But regulation is necessary, in my view, when a handful of firms are able to keep prices at unreasonably high levels, degrade the quality of customer safety and service, and stifle innovation and choice. It is also necessary in any industry that has been created, or substantially benefited, by government and for which there are virtually insurmountable barriers to entry.

In short, I believe the rush to deregulation of broadcasting has been an affront to the public interest and the product of political pressure by the powerful rather than rational analysis by the thoughtful.

Ah, you say, but aren't there a lot more choices today – even before one considers the Internet?

And you'd be right – but only in a very limited sense.

In the 1920s there were less than 1000 stations; now there are over 10,000. In the 1960s there were three commercial TV networks and a handful of independent stations. Today's cable systems often carry 50 channels or more, and satellite services offer many times that.

So why do I think there's not really more choice? Because we're only counting the number of outputs when the relevant number is the number of inputs.

So long as we permit the company that owns the content (the programming) to also own the conduit (the distribution system – network, cable or satellite dish company) we don't have meaningful choice or diversity.

Even if the 10,000 stations were owned by 10,000 owners, and there was no concentration of media ownership, if they were all licensed to and operated by wealthy, conservative, Republicans, living off of the profits from the sale of advertising on those stations, there wouldn't be that much diversity in their programming. The same would be true if they were all owned by the Catholic Church, or trade unions.

What makes for diversity in programming is diversity in business models: a station (like WNYC) owned by a City; or (like WCFL – for "Chicago Federation of Labor") by a trade union; or funded with donors' contributions and government grants (like NPR); or community licensed stations free of "underwriters'" pressures (like the Pacifica Foundation's WBAI); or "pirate radio stations" operating outside the law and regulations of the FCC.

The number of profit-maximizing, advertiser-supported stations makes little difference to the diversity of their offerings. The number of business models can make an enormous difference.

When I was on the Iowa City Cable Commission in the 1980s we didn't have CNN on our local cable system. I talked to Ted Turner about it. He was then willing to make it available to us at 15 cents per subscriber per month, $1.80 a year. The Iowa City cable subscribers were quite willing to pay that. Now the market theorists will tell us that a willing buyer and a willing seller in the marketplace can contract. But their ideology didn't apply in this case. Because the company that owned the Iowa City cable company did not own CNN at that time and was planning on creating a competitive 24-hour news channel. There was no other cable company to deliver the service. We had a willing buyer and a willing seller and yet there was no meaningful marketplace and no possible transaction.

This point has been either overlooked or ignored by regulators and many commentators as well as they chant their ideological mantra of "marketplace."

On the other hand, so long as there is a firewall of separation between those who control content and those who control the distribution conduits it makes little difference how much of a monopoly is held by either. For example, there were few free speech complaints when ATT controlled the entire phone ("distribution") system from handset to long distance lines. Why? Because (a) anyone who wanted a phone could have a phone, and (b) once they got it they could say anything they wanted over the phone. There was a total separation of content and conduit.

The Internet: Origins and the New World Disorder

You may know the story, modeled on a science fiction short story, of the fellow who puts the question to his computer, "Is there a God?" The answer comes back, "Insufficient data." Over time, in a story that can easily take 15 minutes or more to tell, he gradually links more and more computers – in his company, then town, state, and nation. He keeps putting the same question and getting the same answer. Finally, he creates what we today call the Internet. "Is there a God?" he asks. There is a pause and the screen lights up with the answer, "There is now."

However fond I may be of computers even I would not endow them with deistic powers. And I'm fully aware that many believe them the creation of the Devil. Whatever your judgment on that question may be, I think we'd all have to agree the Internet has created what might be called, to play on former President Bush's phrase, "A new world disorder."

As you know, the Internet has been around in one form or another since the 1960s.

There's a certain irony in the fact that the American military, thought to be one of the world's most hierarchical, command and control organizations, created one of the least hierarchical, least controllable, flattest organizations ever designed. They called it ARPA (later DARPA), for the Defense Department's Advanced Research Planning Agency Network.

The ARPANet was designed to enable DOD personnel, defense contractors and academics to communicate easily with each other on military projects. Why no centralized communications command post?

Because they wanted it to be able to survive a nuclear attack; to provide an enemy no single obvious "headquarters" target; to be able to fix itself and re-route traffic around damage.

In fact, it is this quality of the Internet, the uncontrollability built into its architecture, that creates one of the central issues in its regulation still today. Some early adopters may remember BITNET, the network that provided all academics the same facility. Some said at the time that the B-I-T stood for "because it's there."

But what's there now, as we all know, is something called the Internet, complete with the World Wide Web, video, audio, still pictures, voice phone service, online games, music CDs, multi-billion-dollar electronic commerce, and access to billions of pages of information.

It is an inter-connected network of networks (an Inter-Net), just as the interstate highway system is an inter-connected network of highways (an Inter-State). And, although half of the users and facilities are still in the U.S., it is increasingly becoming a truly global communications network, offering every form of media we have ever known before.

Bits and Bytes and Copyrights

In a pre-digital, industrial age, every form of media was both unique and extraordinarily expensive to copy – newspapers, books, phonograph records, photos, and movies. Unless copying was done by hand it required the availability of expensive equipment – printing plants, record pressing facilities, cameras and darkrooms.

Three things have happened since then.

(a) The 99.9%-off sale. We're used to 50%-off sales; not 90%, 99% or 99.9%-off sales. But recent years have brought orders of magnitude reductions in the price of the equipment necessary for copyright violations: VCRs dropped in price from $200,000 to $200 or less; computers from $3,000,000 to $3,000 to close to $300; what formerly required a printing plant costing $200,000 or more can now be accomplished with a $100 scanner and $100 printer.

(b) Digitization. When everything is bits and bytes the copying is not only standardized, simplified and virtually free, it is also a 100% perfect copy every time.

(c) Distribution via the global Internet now makes it easy to move illegal copies of copyrighted material around the planet in an instant by means of file sharing, posting to a Web site, or attaching to an e-mail.

No one has repealed our copyright laws – in fact the terms have been extended over the years. But notwithstanding those laws we still have DVDs and videotapes of Hollywood movies on the streets of Beijing, Singapore and Moscow before they even make it to our movie theaters.

The illegal U.S. businesses that produce those multi-billion-dollar losses for our motion picture and music companies risk prosecution – though they seem hard to close down. But enforcing the law elsewhere is virtually impossible. In some contexts industry and government have simply given up the attempt. The U.S. law authorizes kids to make copies – for their own use only – of the music they have paid for or copied off the radio. Most computer software licenses now permit the equivalent.

And copyright is just one example of what has happened to old laws assaulted by new technologies.

A Government of Engineers and Not of Lawyers

Broadcasting is regulated as much by laws of physics as by laws of Congress. When the FCC addresses the selection of bands and frequencies for various services; the communities of license; directional antennas; a station's transmitting power; antenna height; transmission mode (AM, FM); an "orbital slot" for a communications satellite; or the availability of an FM sub-carrier for data – it must look to science as much or more than law. Those decisions, in turn, affect the choices of technology and services offered to the public, the content of programming, and the cost of receivers – a not insignificant expense – in fact, the largest investment in broadcasting equipment is that of the audience not the broadcasters.

Although many of the decisions have not as directly involved government, and tend to be less obvious than antenna towers, the same thing is true of the Internet. It's sometimes referred to as the distinction between "West coast code" (the software from Silicon Valley) and "East coast code" (the laws and regulations from Washington, D.C.).

The following kinds of things are largely (if not entirely) controlled by "West coast code."

- The "filters" available to parents, schools, libraries, ISPs, corporations, and governments for blocking unwanted content
- The ability to send anonymous messages (or not)
- How much personal data is gathered by the Web pages you visit: name, address, e-mail, demographic data from others with whom you do business
- Who gets to read your e-mail and know what Web pages you've visited
- Who gets access to what material; accounts and passwords vs. open access
- The availability of encryption and its effectiveness
- Information providers' ability to offer material that can be accessed by Internet users (the content and conduit issues)

We don't think of such things as "regulation" – which we associate with government, acts of Congress and FCC regulations – but just as surely they are.

Proposals and Conclusion

One of broadcasting's most admired journalists was Edward R. Murrow. He made an observation about the future of his industry that is equally applicable to those we have today.

His point was that the magic of the new technologies – he was talking about the move from radio to television – lies not within the technology but within ourselves. It is we who must see technology's dangers as well as the opportunities. Otherwise, as he said of television, "it is just lights and wires in a box."

With today's communications technologies the box and wires are ever so much smaller, but the dangers and opportunities are much bigger. However, the responsibility lies in exactly the same place as it did in Edward R. Murrow's day. With us.

I don't think we need a lot of regulation, but we do need some.

For example, just as there is a growing gap between the incomes of the top one percent of the American population and all the rest of us, so there is a digital divide between the information poor and the information rich.

Those of us interested in K-12 education have a bumper sticker that says, "If you think education is expensive just wait until you start paying for ignorance."

What regulation do we need to insure that everyone can benefit from the Information Age? This is a need perceived by those espousing all political ideologies; liberals because it's humane and just, something we owe each other; conservatives because they need employees capable of making them even richer still: clerks who can make change, mechanics who can read the manuals, and assembly line workers who can manage computers.

There's a lot of loose talk about how the Internet makes it possible for everyone on Earth to have access to all human knowledge. Let's look at the facts.

According to the Federal Reserve, during the three years prior to 2000 the average net worth of families earning under $10,000 a year actually *decreased* by 25% to $3,600. If you're curious that's about how much Bill Gates' net worth *increased* – every hour, 24 hours a day, 365 days a year.

The poorest one-fifth saw their net worth decline by 25%. The richest one-fifth saw their average net worth increase over that same three-year period by 22.4% to $1.7 million – nearly 500 times as much

Not surprisingly, these disparities in wealth are reflected in the financial ability to participate in the Information Age according to the National Telecommunications and Information Administration.

About 75% of the central city poor have phones. For those earning over $75,000 a year it's closer to 99%.

One is reminded of Lilly Tomlin's observation regarding the marketing genius behind the idea of selling snack foods in the Third World – those who haven't been able to eat regular meals had not formerly even imagined the concept of between-meal snacks.

Similarly, those without phones represent an enormous untapped market for the sale of modems and broadband Internet access by cable or DSL: the purchase has simply never occurred to them.

Fewer than 10% of those earning under $10,000 a year have computers. For those earning over $75,000 the percentage is above 75%.

Less than 4% of the poor have online service; roughly half of those earning over $75,000 do.

And as our leaders like to remind us, ours is one of the wealthiest nations on earth. So how are the rest of the world's people doing?

Most of our fellow humans have never made a phone call. They don't have electricity. They may be living on less than $200 a year.

It is ludicrous, insensitive and unbelievably myopic to talk about how "everybody" now has access to the billions of documents on the Internet and Web. They don't.

Nor are wealth and infrastructure the only limitations. There's also the matter of education.

You know the expression, "Give a man a fish and he can eat for a day, teach him how to fish and he can eat for a lifetime." Note that the lifetime fish diet comes, not from the fishing pole but from learning, from knowledge, from skill.

Knowing that, you will also not be surprised to learn of the disparity in access to the Information Age between those with the least education and those with a college degree.

Of those with less than a high school diploma fewer than 10% have a computer – compared with about two-thirds of those with a B.A. degree.

There is an even greater spread with regard to online service. About 2% of those with the least education are hooked up, compared with almost 40% of the college educated.

Once again, from a global perspective, bear in mind that every year there are more illiterate people on earth than there were the year before. Not only has our vaunted marketplace approach not solved the problem, it's actually getting worse year by year.

And reflect on the fact that, in part because of the American domination of the Internet, English is its almost universal language.

So imagine for a moment that this "everyone" we talk about did have the financial resources, access to an Internet connection, and the desire and leisure time to utilize an online computer. Unless they know the English language, and have a relatively advanced level of education, they will not be able to use that computer for much more than a doorstop – if they have a door.

Humankind has done a fairly respectable job of making it possible for everyone to participate in the Agricultural Age, the Industrial Age, and then the Services Age. Whether it's done with "the marketplace" or with "regulation," bringing everyone along into the Information Age is one of the most challenging tasks our species has ever confronted.

Content and Conduit

We cannot mandate that all intellectual property be made available for no charge to anyone who wants it. But we can mandate that there not be artificial barriers to access by users (with, of course, exceptions to preserve personal privacy, national security, and corporate proprietary information).

Such Internet content "filters" as there may be should be known to the user, available as an option for parents, and not imposed on those who neither need nor want them.

We cannot mandate that every carrier carry every content provider's information for no charge. But we can insist that they make access available to all providers for equal charges and with equal quality of service.

Personal Privacy

At a minimum we should be told what information is being obtained about us, how it is to be used, and whether it will be shared or sold to others.

We should be asked if we wish to opt in to such a system; at a minimum we should be provided a meaningful opportunity to opt out.

We should have the ability to see what is being recorded and shared about us, and to modify it and correct errors.

"Media Regulation in the Age of the Internet"

We are talking about a sector of our economy, our lives and our culture in which most of the components and qualities are constantly changing.

There are a variety of different needs for regulation, and means of achieving those ends.

But, to the extent the current evidence is an accurate forecast of what's to come, it seems clear that the marketplace is incapable, alone, of getting us there.

(b) Regulating the Cyber-Journalist

This is a paper presented to "The Journalist in Cyberspace Conference," A Warsaw Journalism Center International Conference held at the Palace of Culture in Warsaw, Poland, October 11-12, 1997. It was co-organized and co-sponsored by the Goethe Institute, the Polish National Broadcast Council, the German Embassy, and the American Embassy.

Introduction: The Uniqueness of Polish Journalism

Are there aspects of journalism and the new technologies – the Internet in particular – that require governmental "regulation"?

The shortest answer, and one preferred by many, would be a simple "No."

But law professors do not give short and simple answers, and besides I've been told to take 20 minutes for this presentation. So permit me to elaborate a bit.

To clarify my purpose at the outset, these remarks are, necessarily, drawn from American, rather than Polish, experience.

All Americans have at least some knowledge of Polish history, the struggles you have endured over the past 1000 years, your cultural achievements that have enriched us all, and the substantial contributions great Polish leaders have provided to Poland, America and the world – among others, currently the Pope for the world's Roman Catholics, and until his retirement last week, the Chairman of the Joint Chiefs of Staff of the United States' military forces.

The 1990s have been only the latest period of growth and achievement for your country.

So a major reason for my being here is my desire to learn from you: your system of mass media, how you provide for independent journalism, and the ways in which the government relates to media.

My reluctance to make recommendations comes both from my relative lack of understanding of, and because of the respect I have for, the uniqueness that is Polish journalism.

I will simply describe some of my thoughts and experiences with U.S. government regulation of the media, and some of the issues we are currently confronting in America regarding the Internet. If you find any of it useful you are free to apply it in your own unique way. If you do not find it applicable, hopefully you will at least find it interesting.

If you would like to pursue any of these issues at greater length, I will be around for the entire conference. After that I am available to you on the Internet.

Convergence and Cyberspace

"Convergence" is a current buzz-word in discussions of the current, and future, state of media. So there is nothing original in my mentioning it. But a brief word on the subject may be necessary to put these remarks in context.

When I was serving as a commissioner of the U.S. Federal Communications Commission, some twenty-five years ago, the categories were clear.

The most casual observer would have no difficulty distinguishing a telephone from a television set – or a radio transmitter.

The product of newspaper journalists was manufactured with printers' ink and newsprint and delivered by trucks.

There was no confusing the companies, wires, or content brought to the home by the cable television company and the phone company.

The FCC's regulatory efforts were carried out by bureaus bearing the name of the industries in question – the "Common Carrier Bureau," the "Broadcast Bureau."

Today, seemingly everything is converging.

Global media conglomerates are merging print, broadcast, satellite and cable television distribution – along with film and television program production.

Newspapers, today, deliver their content not only on newsprint, but also by fax and e-mail, voice phone access, cable channels – and the Web. In fact, that's how I can get current issues of the *Warsaw Voice* delivered to my home computer.

Telephone companies want to get into the cable television business, cable companies want to get into the phone business, local phone companies want to provide long distance, and long distance carriers want to provide local phone and data services – and the Congress has encouraged all of it with the Telecommunications Act of 1996.

Pagers, cell phones and "palm top" computers are coming to perform similar functions – and even look alike.

The same satellite technology that brings television programs, and is called DirectTV, can also bring high speed Internet access, and is called Direct PC.

At this point it is not yet clear whether the television set is going to end up being our primary access to the Web ("WebTV") as well as to television programs, or whether the Internet is going to provide our primary access to what we today call "television" – along with the Web.

The FCC now has a "Mass Media Bureau" instead of a "Broadcast Bureau."

Thus, we are today living through a confusing convergence of technologies, services, industries, and regulation that may make our emphasis on "journalism in cyberspace" a somewhat narrow, arbitrary and unrealistic focus.

The only two things we probably know for sure are that (1) something like what we today think of as journalism is going to continue to provide some of the input into tomorrow's "Infocosm" (if I may borrow Andersen Consulting's word). And (2) that Infocosm will be filled, and drawn upon, with a seamless web of technologies, services, companies and individuals.

William Gibson, who gave us the word "cyberspace" in the 1984 book *Neuromancer*, was using it to describe what we would, today, more likely refer to as "virtual reality" – a realistic, electronic, artificial "environment" in three dimensions, stimulating all the senses.

Today "cyberspace" is used in a variety of ways, but often interchangeably with "the Internet" or "Web."[1]

So however artificial a focus on cyberspace in a converging world may be, and however far our current meaning has drifted from that of Mr. Gibson, that will be my limited focus, and definition. Otherwise, the topic expands to impossible lengths – not unlike the famous professorial essay question: "Describe the universe and give two examples."

The First Amendment: The Presumption of No Regulation

As you probably know, the original constitutions for Poland and the United States came into existence about the same time – 1789 and 1791.

Our Constitution has been amended many times since, but the First Amendment is, in some ways, the best known and the most important of those amendments.

It provides, "Congress shall make no law . . . abridging the freedom of speech or of the press . . .."

Although this language is fairly clear, it is also quite general. Its precise meaning and application have been spelled out by the decisions reached by U.S. courts over the past 200 years.

Essential to an understanding of how that works is awareness of the independence of U.S. federal judges. Appointed by the President and approved by the Senate, once in office they are there for life – with no allegiance to political parties or Executive or Legislative Branch officials.[2]

What is "Journalism"?

At the outset, we are confronted with defining "journalism," and "the media."

In rejecting the notion that the First Amendment's reference to "or of the press" confers any rights on the mass media beyond those of "freedom of speech," one Supreme Court justice commented on the difficulty of defining "the press." If the definition is limited to the likes of *The New York Times* and CNN, it thereby excludes the only "press" known to those who drafted the First Amendment: the small circulation publications of individual owner-editors. On the other hand, if such publications are included within the definition, it includes so much as to be virtually indistinguishable from the "speech" of private citizens that may include letters-to-the-editor, or multi-copy handbills.

The Internet only exacerbates this problem. Take my own Web page as an example. I post the full text of most of my writings and interviews. Some of what I post are opinion columns written for major newspapers. But I may also post material – such as the text for these remarks – which has never been published in a conventional sense elsewhere. Is the former "journalism" and the latter not?

There is, of course, a problem for the Web surfer, the reader – or the journalist using the Internet for research. In some ways it's not different from the problems when evaluating print. How reliable is this source, this writer? Are they writing from an ideological, propaganda perspective? How thorough is their research? The mere fact that something is communicated in print, on paper, does not make it true or useful. But print, whether books, magazines or newspapers, usually involves at least some "gate-keeping" function by somebody. On the Internet, anybody can become his or her own reporter, editor and publisher.

No less distinguished a journalist than Pierre Salinger – former press secretary to Presidents Kennedy and Johnson, and an able ABC reporter – may have been a victim of these qualities of the Internet. He charged that a U.S. military missile was, in fact, the cause of the crash of a commercial airliner in waters off New York City. There was a Web page presenting precisely this theory. Unfortunately, it was put together by someone who didn't really think it made any difference whether the report was fact or fiction – as long as it made a good story.

We can say that nothing on the Internet is journalism, or that all of it is, or that some is and some isn't. It probably makes more sense to look at it on a case-by-case basis, depending on the purpose.

Restrictions Applicable to All – Including Journalists

To say that we do not license journalists, and that we have few, if any, laws or regulations applicable to journalists, does not mean that they are left outside the law.

For the most part, laws generally applicable to all citizens in the U.S. are also applicable to journalists. For example, although the Congress has provided special tax exempt status for religious organizations, it has provided none for the media.

Newspapers and broadcast stations must pay income taxes like any other business; journalists must pay personal income taxes like every other citizen. If someone goes on another's property without permission that is a legal (civil) offense called "trespass." When a journalist goes on someone's property to take a photograph, or otherwise get a story, he or she is just as subject to a law suit for trespass as anyone else (with some limited exceptions). Even though a reporter is in a hurry to get a story back to the newspaper or station he or she is subject to the same traffic laws as anyone else.

In fact, most of the "regulation of journalism" in the United States is of just this kind – regulation that applies to every business and citizen, everything from antitrust to zoning.

Journalists' Special Privileges

Just as there are few, if any, regulations of journalists, neither are there, for the most part, special privileges.

Indeed, many journalists oppose the idea of special privilege on the grounds that with special privileges from government may come special obligations or restrictions. Sometimes called "The Fourth Estate," representatives of the media like to rely on the First Amendment as evidence of their total independence from government.

Notwithstanding these protestations, however, there is the legal question of whether the Constitution's reference to "or of the press" adds anything to the "freedom of speech" possessed by the media equally with all citizens. There is some basis for arguing that it does.

The U.S. Supreme Court has held, for example, that the media should have some First Amendment protection from the laws of libel – lest fear of large damage actions might "chill" the inclination of media owners fully to report about public matters.

At least some justices believe that reporters should have a First Amendment-based privilege to maintain the confidentiality of their sources – in circumstances in which a private citizen would have to testify, say, before a grand jury.

The Supreme Court refused to permit the Executive Branch's efforts to prevent *The New York Times* from publishing classified government documents about the Viet Nam War that had been stolen from the Pentagon – under circumstances in which a private citizen probably would have been jailed.

Reporters' "press passes" may get them into the White House, the Congressional "press gallery," private meetings, or behind police barricades at the scenes of accidents or fires when private citizens would be barred.

The Post Office has, for years, provided subsidized, low rates for the distribution of newspapers and magazines.

For the most part, however, journalists have no rights beyond those of all citizens to, for example, get access to government documents under the "Freedom of Information Act," tour prisons and other government buildings, and attend trials or other official, public meetings.

Journalism in Cyberspace: The Similarities

If journalists have neither special regulations nor privileges, and we even have difficulty defining "journalism," our inquiry into the regulation of "journalism in cyberspace" becomes, simply, an inquiry into government regulation of the Internet/Web in general.

There are, of course, laws and regulations resulting from the uniqueness that is cyberspace – the Internet, the Web – and we will address those shortly. But, once again, for the most part the laws applicable in cyberspace are the same laws applicable everywhere else.

Defamation – libel and slander – is little different in cyberspace from what it is when printed in a newspaper or spray-painted on the side of a barn.

To the extent that "obscenity" or "indecency" are regulated generally, they are also regulated in cyberspace.

Fraud, or what we call "false and misleading advertising," is subject to the same legal standards.

Privacy rights exist in cyberspace as elsewhere. The law of copyright is equally applicable.

To the extent a professional journalist feels constrained by principles of journalistic ethics she should feel equally constrained whether communicating in cyberspace or in hard copy print.

So, for the most part, to the extent there are laws governing journalism in any medium they will also be applicable to journalism in cyberspace.

Journalism in Cyberspace: The Differences

One of the most obvious differences between cyberspace and print involves geography.

We have legal systems that have operated on a centuries-old unstated assumption that they apply within arbitrary (and, as you well know, changing) political boundaries on Planet Earth – nations, their subdivisions, and cities.

"The law" is the federal law of a nation, or the local law of a state.

A court has "jurisdiction" over those citizens who live within its political boundaries.

A person has a legal "domicile" – usually where they live. Lawyers and doctors are licensed to practice their profession by a state – and can only practice within that state. Even in today's "global economy," most businesses are still identified with the country where their headquarters are located. Judges and lawyers don't talk about geography very much, but it is the foundation on which most law and regulation are based.

Cyberspace, by definition, is not geographically bound. Geography is simply irrelevant. Someone whose computer is connected to the Internet, the Web, is attached to a global network of computers. The net effect (if you'll pardon the pun) is that they have, thereby, created the equivalent of taking all the files in all the computers on Planet Earth and putting them on the hard drive of their desktop or laptop computer. Click on a link and a new screen of material appears – just as if it was one of their files. The computer on which that new screen of material is stored may be in Poland, Japan, Chile, South Africa, or the United States. The location of that computer, and the countries (or satellites) through which its data travels, are not only irrelevant, they are often unknown to the user.

How does this affect the law, the regulation, of cyberspace? A legal action for defamation involves consideration of the extent to which the plaintiff's reputation has been harmed in her or his "community." What is the relevant community for someone defamed on the Internet? The city or neighborhood where they live – or work? The entire world of people with access to the Web? Those with whom the plaintiff communicates through e-mail, news groups, and Web pages?

Similarly, "obscenity," as defined by the U.S. Supreme Court, involves a number of elements. But a part of the definition refers to "contemporary community standards." Once again, what is the "community"? Where the defendant lives? Where the computer is located on which the questionable material is stored? The "community" of people who regularly download material from his Web site? Any and every sensitive community around the world from which one could get access to the Web page?[3]

In order to have "jurisdiction" over a party, courts usually require that the party have some contact with the geographical area where the court sits, for example, a state. The party may live there, or have a business there, or send sales persons into the area. Is it enough that the party – who lives and works outside of the state – stores material on a computer within the state? Is it enough that the party's Web page is available to people living within the state? If so, that would mean that anyone who posts something on the Web is subject to jurisdiction in every court on earth.

Cyberspace not only turns geographically-based legal systems upside down, the inherent technology of computers and their networks puts enormous strains on something like copyright law.

When printing presses were huge, expensive industrial items, and there were few of them, citizens and governments alike knew who was likely to have illegally copied someone else's material.

Today, young children often have access to all the equipment necessary to make illegal copies of musical recordings, computer software, TV shows and video tapes. Anything on the Web can be copied – onto a disk, or printed out; or sent and "published" elsewhere

– with the click of a mouse. None of this changes the law of copyright, but it certainly changes the capacity for violating, and the difficulties in enforcement, of that law. As a result, one of today's hot cyberspace law topics is the future of copyright.

The Internet was first settled by Wild West cowboys primarily interested in selflessly contributing and downloading information and computer software as a contribution to the online community. The Information Superhighway was seen as an adventurer's foot path, not a paved road to riches. Now that the major global media conglomerates are becoming players they want to make money from everything they put on the Web. They have thereby changed the cooperative spirit of the online community in the process. They are meeting resistance with this clash of cultures. But you may be aware of the meeting in Geneva December 1996 at which 160 countries agreed to many of the global media conglomerates' requests.

Cyberspace Regulation: Some Current U.S. Issues

To the extent we want to focus on anything having to do with the Internet that may involve law, regulation, or standard setting – rather than just "journalism" – there are, of course, many topics.

Some of the areas that might be identified would include:

- the jurisdictional issues mentioned above
- online gambling (originating in states or nations where it is legal but, via the Internet, available in states where it is not)
- restrictions on free speech (mentioned above in the context of regulations of obscenity and indecency), both laws of general applicability and those specifically directed at Internet speech
- copyright protection, also mentioned above
- crimes, or threats, involving personal security: pedophiles contacting children by way of the Internet, sexual harassment or stalking
- economic crimes: theft of passwords or credit card numbers, breaking into computers ("hacking"), fraudulent schemes of various kinds, securities fraud (sales of stock over the Internet)

- economic regulation: protection of trademarks and trade names in the selection, registration and protection of domain names (*e.g.*, "ibm.com")
- rights to "link" from one site to another; "framing" (Can linking be prohibited, or charged for, when one site provides a link to a second site, but includes the advertising from the first site?)
- "spamming" (sending out "electronic junk mail" to massive lists)
- privacy issues: collecting data from users, both voluntarily contributed and clandestinely acquired; providing online access to compilations of data about individuals otherwise hard to acquire (such as drivers' license records); monitoring users' (students; employees) e-mail; the "Clipper Chip" (providing citizens the security of encryption for financial or other private transactions – but leaving open a "back door" enabling government agents to break the code)
- the gap between the "information rich and information poor"
- hardware and training for self defense: screening software that blocks an individual's (or their children's) access to designated Web sites, or material from home, schools, or public libraries; the so-called "V chip" to enable parents to program their TV sets

Of course, any journalist, or media outlet, that puts material on the Internet is affected by some of these issues.

But the primary persons and businesses affected are: those using the Internet to get information – sometimes called "netizens" (as in "citizens of the Net"); the schools and universities that provide a significant proportion of the computer accounts, hardware, and networks; Internet service providers – whether large companies with national reach or small local companies; software companies, such as Netscape, and Microsoft (Internet Explorer); hardware manufacturers: personal computers, satellite dishes, phone and cable companies; the carriers that provide the netizens with access to the Internet service providers .

To the extent the journalist, or media owner, is also in any of these categories, he or she is equally subject to whatever regulations may be applicable.

Conclusion

This is an exciting time, but also a confusing time, for those of us interested in the subject of regulation of journalism in cyberspace. Society generally tends to lag behind the scientists and engineers. As someone has observed, it took the university professors forty years just to get the overhead projector out of the bowling alleys and into the classrooms. Half of the world's population has yet to make its first telephone call. Only a small proportion has computers. And fewer still have online access to e-mail and the World Wide Web.

Lawyers and politicians tend to lag behind society. As the old saying goes, "If the people will lead, their leaders will follow." Law professors are supposed to train future lawyers in a skill called "spotting the issues." It is, of course, a necessary preliminary to coming up with public policy proposals. And such proposals must be discussed over time before a consensus will emerge that can form the basis for legislation – or other social standards.

At this point in history we are still trying to spot the issues. There are few efforts at new legislation – and some of those have been found to violate our constitutional protection of free speech. There are relatively few judicial opinions. And many of those represent little more than efforts to pour familiar, decades-old wine into new, electronic bottles. Eventually, in my view, we will need to do what they sometimes say in Hollywood: "Take it from the top." Start all over. Re-think a legal system for a world without geography, a technology without nationality.

And when we do, if it is to be effective, it seems to me inevitable that it will have to be a global effort.

Perhaps our discussions today can be a start.

Endnotes

1. "Cyberspace," for these purposes, includes, of course, a number of distinguishable systems of communication:

> e-mail from one person to one, or very few recipients

> e-mail distributed to a great many unwilling individuals as "electronic junk mail" ("spam")

> list serves that "publish" messages, documents (or online newspapers and magazines, "e-zines") to groups of individuals who have requested the material; usually "edited" in some fashion, a list serve can also automatically re-distribute material from its "subscribers" back out to the list

> newsgroups (now some 15,000 world wide) that maintain (for a time) the entries of those who share a common interest and wish to access the discussion

> use of a remote computer (with or without an account), as with "ftp" (file transfer protocol), "telnet," or "gopher" – or, for that matter, the Web

> real time interactive communication (as distinguished from a-synchronous e-mail), such as "Internet Relay Chat," "Instant Messaging," or "Text Messaging"

2. For a fuller explanation of the workings of the First Amendment see, "An Autonomous Media," Chapter 1 (a).

3. For a Supreme Court definition of "obscenity," see *Miller v. California*, 413 U.S. 15 (1973). A case that illustrates the geography problem involved a couple who lived, and kept their computer, in Northern California – where the material they made available might very well have not been found obscene – who were convicted on the basis of "contemporary community standards" in Memphis, Tennessee – where someone downloaded some of their files. *U.S. v. Thomas*, 74 F.2d 701 (6th Cir. 1996).

Chapter Ten: Intellectual Property Issues in a Digital Universe

(a) How to Violate Copyright Without Actually Copying Anything

This op ed column was published by The Gazette, July 10, 2005. It was a response to a Gazette editorial of July 1, 2005, "Stop Bumming Your Music," to which reference is made in this column. Subsequently, The Gazette published a letter from Aaron Larson, "Keep on Rockin' In the Free World." Larson is a musician who gives away his music on the Internet, an example of one of the legitimate uses of "file sharing" to which the op ed column referred.

The U.S. Supreme Court's opinions are available as Metro-Goldwyn-Mayer Studios v. Grokster, 545 U.S. 913 (2005), and Sony v. Universal City Studios, Inc., 464 U.S. 417 (1984).

The *Gazette*'s right that in this digital era of the Information Age, copyright does indeed create "one of the trickiest moral and ethical dilemmas of this new century."

Sufficiently tricky dilemmas that neither the editorial, nor this column, will resolve them.   The dilemma confronting U.S. Supreme Court justices and *Gazette* editorial writers in the *Grokster* case was that the defendant had not copied anything.

"Grokster" is original, innovative computer software. Apparently, its creators never copied music unlawfully. Never sold or gave away illegally copied music. Never had it on their computers. So why were they violating copyright laws? Lower courts didn't think they were. The issue was whether they were guilty of "vicarious" or "contributory" copyright violations. That's legalese for "Gotcha, even though you didn't copy anything."

The *Gazette* wrote, "What Grokster is doing is wrong. And by extension, those illegally downloading copyrighted songs are wrong, too." The *Gazette* got it backward. The music industry's greed and unimaginative business models have contributed to its problems. Nonetheless, making copies of songs without the copyright owner's permission is wrong. Offering those illegal copies to others for sale or free is wrong. Those are copyright violations. But the folks violating the law by downloading music weren't sued. Grokster was.

The *Gazette* merely asserted that what Grokster did was wrong. But that was the central issue before the court. Can what Grokster did be a copyright violation, "by extension," because those who did violate the copyright law used Grokster's software? Lots of equipment can facilitate copyright violations — including the *Gazette*'s printing press. To facilitate British royal censorship, until 1694 the Crown granted favored printers monopoly licenses. Once the monopolies were repealed, anyone with a press could copy others' books. Printers lobbied for what we'd recognize as copyright protection, the 1707 Statute of Anne. This is more than a historical footnote. Printing presses worldwide are still today producing books for which the copyright owner receives no royalties.

If Grokster's software is illegal just because it can be used in others' copyright violations, should The *Gazette*'s printing press also be outlawed? What about machine copiers, fax machines, audio and video tape recorders, computers generally, especially those with CD and DVD burners? Should their manufacture be prohibited? The publishing, film and music industries have been arguing this for years.

In the *Sony* case, the movie industry claimed all VCRs were copyright violations. The Supreme Court disagreed. It said that recording a TV program to watch later was legitimate. Sure, it acknowledged, some purchasers will sometimes use VCRs in ways that violate copyright. But manufacturers shouldn't be liable "by extension" if the equipment has substantial non-infringing uses. Does file-sharing software have legitimate, non-infringing uses? Absolutely. The court noted its advantages of "security, cost, and efficiency" for "universities, government agencies, corporations and libraries." Even the music industry benefits, as new music groups give away music to become better known.

No, Grokster's downfall didn't come because the software failed to meet the *Sony* test. It was because the company was inducing, and marketing its use for, copyright violations. As users increased, so did Grokster's advertising revenue. The constitutional purpose for copyright is "to promote progress in science and the useful arts." Monopoly rights for owners are a means, not an end. The drafters wanted to promote the social progress resulting from our use of, and building upon, others' intellectual property.

Those who make, offer, or download illegal copies of copyrighted music violate the law. Those who do not copy, but manufacture devices primarily designed and marketed to promote others' illegal copying also may be guilty.

The challenge lies in striking the balance between encouraging technological and intellectual progress on the one hand, and preventing theft on the other. Innovative business models make it possible. The recording industry is slowly learning that lesson.

(b) Copyright, Fair Use, and Blogging

This portion of Chapter 10 is an edited version of what first appeared as a blog entry in FromDC2Iowa.blogspot.com: "Copyright, Fair Use, Blogging & Other Items," July 13, 2007.

We are about to lose a very creative and productive blogger from the blogosphere [July 2007]. It appears that his decision to close down the blog may have been prompted by an intimidating threat of legal action from an Iowa newspaper.

I don't know what the facts are beyond what the blogger has reported. I don't know the paper's side of the story, and I've never communicated with or even known the identity of the anonymous blogger. As we used to say in Texas, "I don't have a dog in this fight," and I'm deliberately not identifying the parties.

The blogger reprints the email from the newspaper. Here are some excerpts:

> "You may link to our site, but you cannot post more than 3-4 sentences of the story on your site.
>
> As the copyright owner of that article, [the paper] has the exclusive right to its reproduction and distribution. We therefore ask that you immediately remove the posted article

from your website and cease any and all further use of the material. Any continued posting or use will be considered willful copyright infringement.

Within 24 hours of your receipt of this email, you should . . . [confirm] that: . . . 2) you will not engage in any further unauthorized copying of [this newspaper's] materials.

If you do not take the steps outlined above, this matter will be turned over to our attorneys for further action."

I don't want to get into a lengthy legal analysis about this for a variety of reasons. (a) Even – or perhaps especially – from the perspective of the newspaper I think it's in no one's best interest to make a federal case out of this. The issues I find most interesting, and significant, are other than "legal" in the usual sense. (b) If it were to become a legal case the outcome would turn on an interpretation of the "Fair Use" doctrine – which is notoriously ambiguous and difficult to predict and apply (though my instinct is that the blogger in question is well within its protections). (c) It doesn't make a lot of sense, as the old saying has it, "to get in a fight with someone who buys printer's ink by the barrel."

But a little legal background is necessary to understand the non-legal issues.

Copyright law, with its foundation in the Constitution, is expressed in terms of both an "end" and a "means."

Article I, Section 8 of the Constitution provides that the end, purpose, or goal is "to promote the progress of science and useful arts." A *means* for accomplishing that end, one of the ways in which that progress is promoted, is to make the products of science and useful arts widely available.

How does that promote such progress? By enabling others to utilize and build upon that prior work of others. An historian can draw upon prior historical accounts as well as research in original documents. Novelists and playwrights use the story lines and themes from earlier novels and plays. Inventors are able to improve upon prior inventions. Songwriters can write lyrics that parody earlier songs. Scientific research can begin with a survey of pre-existing literature. Reviews of works can draw upon their content. Opinion pieces can flourish.

So one of the very purposes of copyright law, ironically, is to encourage what might appear to some to be a "copyright violation" – namely, using all or portions of another's work without permission or payment.

Plagiarism is, of course, another matter: the use of another's work without attribution. To use the work of another without attribution would always be plagiarism, but would not always be a copyright violation if, for example, the plagiarist actually held a license from the copyright owner, or used a sufficiently small portion to be characterized as "Fair Use."

In contrast to the intended "end" of copyright law, the "means" for accomplishing this end chosen by the Constitution's drafters was "by securing for limited times to authors . . . the exclusive right to their respective writings . . .."

In other words, the general rule was that the product of all creative work was to be available to future creators in order that they might be able to make further progress in science and useful arts. This available work was described as being "in the public domain."

The exception to the general rule was that, to help encourage creativity, for a "limited time" after its creation the creator would have the "exclusive right" to use – and therefore to charge others for their use of the work. This exclusive right is called "copyright."

Of course, a problem potentially arises when the "exclusive right" conflicts with the overall purpose of copyright law to "promote progress." That is, when the copyright owner refuses to let others make any use at all of her work – or sets the price for doing so at such high levels as to foreclose use – the "means" defeats the "end" of copyright.

Enter "Fair Use," now found in the Copyright Act in Sec. 107, embodying an earlier doctrine from the common law. The "Fair Use" doctrine mentions four factors to be considered in deciding whether a given unauthorized use of copyrighted works is permissible as "Fair Use."

It is this multiple-variable analysis that contributes to making predictions of Fair Use cases outcomes difficult. The amount used, and whether it is a fictional or non-fictional work are mentioned. But the most important factors go to the economic impact of the use. Is it for "commercial" gain, or for noncommercial "criticism, comment" or "nonprofit educational purposes"? Finally, what is the effect of the use on the "potential market" for the work?

Suppose someone were to sell memberships to, or profit from advertising on, a Web site where, without authorization, they make available every article from every issue of a given newspaper – or the full text of entire books still under copyright. It would be very difficult for the Web site owner to succeed in a law suit with the claim they were engaged in "Fair Use."

The fact that it was news, or non-fiction books, rather than creative fiction would cut in their favor under one of the Fair Use factors. But aside from that, the other three factors would cut against them: they are copying the entire paper, they are profiting from selling access to it, and the hits on their Web site are probably reducing the number of hits on the newspaper's site. It would make their case even weaker if they were doing nothing but reproducing the newspaper – without any original commentary or criticism.

Now consider the blogger in question.

I've already said virtually nothing is a "slam dunk" when it comes to Fair Use. But I really think he has the better of the argument here.

He is clearly involved in commentary, a use which is expressly mentioned in the law.

He is not in the business of selling newspapers – or even individual stories from newspapers. In fact, he's not in any business – and certainly not a "commercial" one that profits from the sale of the newspaper's copyrighted stories or even hits on his blog.

So far as I know, no one – at least not I – go to his site to find out what was in the paper that morning. Indeed it is relevant, I think, that the paper makes the entirety of its content freely available from its own Web site, from which any Web surfer can read, copy, print out, or send by email any story to anyone connected to the Internet anywhere in the world.

Readers of his blog (and he notes there are 25,000 unique visitors every month) are primarily interested in what he calls his "insightfully vulgar" commentary – not the content of what he is commenting about. There are obviously a goodly number of readers who find his commentary entertaining and often very funny (sufficiently so that, if they are not thin skinned, they will even continue reading when he appears to be slaughtering their own sacred cows).

The material he quotes (and he not only attributes his sources, but often includes a link to papers' Web sites), is a statistically insignificant portion of any given morning paper's issue. Seldom (if ever) does he even reproduce an entire story.

The paper's threatening email to the blogger refers to a permitted "3-4 sentence" standard. I know of no such rule. That is, sometimes a single phrase would not be protected by "Fair Use" while under other circumstances an entire work might be.

Finally, the only conceivable economic impact of his blog's use of excerpts from the paper's stories, it seems to me, would be to increase (a) the number of blog readers who go to the paper's Web site (at least some of whom would not otherwise have done so), (b) their inclination to subscribe to, and (c) advertise in, the paper.

In short, while I can see ways in which "the effect of the use on the potential market for . . . the copyrighted work" would be to enhance that market and increase the paper's profits, it is difficult to see how the paper's "potential market" cold be adversely affected by the blog's limited use of material from its stories.

I wouldn't go so far as to say the paper ought to have to pay him for advertising the paper and increasing their readership, but I certainly don't think they are in a position to argue they should have the legal right to close him down because he has harmed them economically.

I can only hope that the paper was not prompted to play its copyright card because of its being upset, not with the use of its stories, but with his legally appropriate and protected (even if "insightfully vulgar") commentary about those stories.

Because – putting aside the fact that it seems to me a real stretch to try to make a case that the blogger is not well within "Fair Use" – it strikes me as unseemly for a newspaper to be curtailing speech by using threats, perhaps intended to but in any event having the effect of, closing down one of America's most popular blogs.

Whatever happened to, "If there be time to expose through discussion the falsehood and fallacies, to avert the evil by the processes of education, the remedy to be applied is more speech, not enforced silence," as Justice Louis Brandeis advised by way of a concurring opinion in *Whitney v. California*, 274 U.S. 357, 377 (1927)?

Newspapers can be proud of their defense of First Amendment rights in this country. But bloggers are now the modern day equivalent of what mainstream newspapers' ancestors looked like 200 or more years ago. The exchange between the mainstream media and the blogosphere has been good for both – and for America. While that relationship is still budding and both are trying to find their way is not the time for us to start threatening, suing and trying to silence each other.

Just some thoughts from the sidelines; my obituary for a blog that now leaves a hole in the blogosphere that does the kind of damage to our intellectual lives that holes in the ozone do to our physical lives. It is especially ironic and sorrowful that such a murder would be committed by a newspaper.

Chapter Eleven: Media and Politics

Media as Politics: What's A Voter to Do?

The material for Chapter 11 has been drawn from a speech text for an address at Earlham College, Richmond, Indiana, September 15, 2004. Much has been deleted, such as a discussion of voting machines and impediments to, and reforms for, third parties – along with dozens of references in footnotes embedded in the original text. The full text and supporting references are available online at: http://www.nicholasjohnson.org/writing/masmedia/earlham.html.

The Problem With the Media

It is the rankest of understatement to say that there are problems with today's mass media.

This observation is no longer limited to media critics like myself.

1. The Pew Research Center released a study earlier this year that surveyed hundreds of the nation's journalists. Over half of those they call national journalists think their profession is headed down the wrong path. Two-thirds think the financial pressures for ever-increasing profits is "seriously hurting" news coverage.

   Understandably, perception is affected by past experience. Of those journalists who have known a better day (those over 55), one-third think loss of credibility is the profession's biggest problem. Only 10% of those under 35 share that view.

2. Mergers of media firms have resulted in the gradual reduction in the number of dominant companies from the 50 we used to have to about six firms that today control roughly 90% of the information, opinion and entertainment we consume.

3. Advertiser pressure has increased. And owners are permitting it to enter the newsroom. Commercially produced video material – such as new model Harley-Davidson motorcycles, or a new color for M&M candy – is inserted into local news programs as if it was news. Product placement is rampant throughout feature films and entertainment television. News stories in anyway critical of any business, let alone advertisers, are more likely to be censored than even proposed.

4. As firms extend their reach by combining all media under one corporate roof – from books, to movies, to television, to video rentals, to newspapers and magazines – they often yield to the financial pressure to ignore the conflicts of interest this creates. They begin to hype their subsidiaries' products. They call it "synergy."

5. In recent years we have had an increase in both the amateurs on the Internet, and the ideologues with little or no journalistic training on the numerous cable channels. It's obviously cheaper to produce shouting matches than reports from foreign correspondents, so that's what they do. But it's not what we used to call journalism.

It's as if facts are no longer relevant.

Los Angeles Times editor, John S. Carroll, tells the following story.

Prior to the California recall election, the *L.A. Times* investigated the stories that now-Governor Arnold Schwarzenegger was a womanizer. In an effort to support Schwarzenegger by discrediting the *Times*, Bill O'Reilly's show on Fox TV,

"embarked on a campaign to convince its audience that . . . [the *Times*] attacked only Republicans and gave Democrats a free ride. . . . Where, he asked, was the *L.A. Times* on the so-called [Clinton] Troopergate story? Why hadn't it sent reporters to Arkansas? How could it justify an investigation of Schwarzenegger's misbehavior with women and not Clinton's?"

In fact, Carroll writes, the *Times* had

> "sent its best reporters there, and it sent them in force. At one point, it had nine reporters in Little Rock. And when two of them wrote the first Troopergate story to appear in any newspaper, they made the *Times* the leader on that subject. Not a leader, but the leader. Their story would be cited frequently as other newspapers tried to catch up."

> As Carroll acknowledges, the problem with Fox, and many of the others, is not that they occasionally make a factual error. That happens at the *Times* as well. The problem is the number that is made, the seeming willingness to accept and repeat factual errors that support an ideological or partisan position, and the almost total unwillingness to publish corrections.

We will return to Fox in a moment. But since we're addressing "the media as politics" perhaps we should leave the media for a moment and turn to politics.

The Struggle for Democracy

True democracy has almost always been resisted by those in power. Most of those said to be the fathers of our democratic system, those who drafted the Declaration of Independence and Constitution, agreed with John Jay that, "Those who own the country, should run it." It is a view still widely held today by those in power.

Recall that at the beginning of our nation women could not vote. African-Americans could not vote. White males who did not own land could not vote. And no one aged 18, 19 or 20 could vote.

When I was going to college in the South in the 1950s voters were taxed. We had to pay to go to the polls. It was called a "poll tax."

Many community and business leaders profited politically and economically by discouraging the poor and working poor from voting.

None of the expansions of the franchise was freely given. Each had to be fought for with grassroots people's movements – from marching in the streets to, in one case, a civil war.

But ultimately these expansions of our democracy were won. We've yet to go so far as Australia and other countries to encourage voting by taxing those who don't vote, but at least we no longer tax those who do.

As a result of this expanding electorate, today's establishment has to be much more inventive in devising ways of holding on to power, including coming up with ways of discouraging the poor from voting.

Efforts to Discourage Voting

There isn't much one can say in favor of the poll tax except for its almost total absence of hypocrisy. It made clear upon its face that its purpose was to significantly discourage, if not prevent, voting by those for whom the expenditure of a dollar or two was a matter calling for some considerable deliberation. Since poverty was disproportionately the lot of southern African-Americans the racist motives of poll tax enthusiasts was also not hidden from view.

Since the repeal of the poll tax, "those who own the country," to quote John Jay once again, have become somewhat less honest in their efforts to limit the franchise to themselves. They simply oppose any and all proposals that might make it easier for the poor and working class to register and vote: leaving the polls open for 24 hours, in fact any effort to extend the hours for voting; a guaranteed right of leave with pay for purposes of voting, or declaring election day a national holiday; making it possible for any citizen to register new voters and help them to vote absentee; more clerks for shorter voter registration lines; early voting at satellite polls in supermarkets and malls; and registration where drivers licenses are issued ("motor voting").

Commission on Presidential Debates

One of the most invidious schemes is the one thing about which virtually all major contributors, Republican and Democratic Party officials agree. There should never, ever, be a crack through which a third party might worm its way into the political arena.

The fact that the two parties control the Commission on Presidential Debates results in its setting the threshold for participation just slightly above whatever is the percentage support of the leading third party.

What does it tell you about the big money control of both of our major political parties that each of them seems equally concerned that they will lose support if voters are permitted to hear anything other than the vacuous platitudes and negative campaign ads they offer us?

What are they afraid of?

They are afraid that if a third party candidate was permitted to discuss the issues that really affect the lives of the poor, working poor, working class and lower middle class, if he or she would describe the corporate welfare payments that make ours a system of socialism for the rich and free private enterprise for the poor, the power of the two major parties and their special interest financiers might begin to erode.

It's a circular, classic "Catch 22." To have the popular support of those considered by the media and public to be "serious candidates" a candidate must participate in the presidential debates. But to participate the debates a candidate must meet the Commission on Presidential Debates' standard for how much popular support you must have before you can participate in their debates.

But the debates are only the most obvious of the war on third parties and an informed electorate.

Ignorance as a Political Tool

Notwithstanding all that has been done to make it difficult for the people to vote, and to remove from their view the candidates of the third parties that might speak to their interests, "those who run the country" are still threatened by the existence of elections and the always present possibility that people will actually show up to vote.

Have you heard of Noam Chomsky? The British *Guardian* has said "Chomsky ranks with Marx, Shakespeare, and the Bible as one of the ten most quoted sources in the humanities." *The New York Times* says he is "arguably the most important intellectual alive."

And yet even if you had been paying attention to American mass media the odds of your ever having heard of Noam Chomsky would be somewhere between slim and none at all. He's not exactly a favorite of the radio and television talk show producers and hosts.

Why might that be? As Noam Chomsky has pointed out in the book and film, *Manufacturing Consent*, in any country in which the government does not have adequate police, military and security forces to completely control what the people *do*, it is necessary to control what the people *think*.

Controlling what the people think, it turns out, is not as difficult as you might imagine.

One tactic is to leave the people uninformed. No less a student of the media than former CBS anchor Walter Cronkite thinks the American people are "dangerously uninformed."

And why might that be? There are those in our country who gain – politically and economically – from widespread public ignorance.

An African-American friend of mine, a disk jockey, told me a story of his first job at a radio station in the south. He was handed a stack of records and told to play them. He asked about the news department and was told by the white male owner there was none. He asked about what was then called a "teletype," a device for bringing AP or other wire service news to radio stations. The station didn't have one of those, either. He tried again, telling the owner that he would just buy the local paper and repeat something of what was in it.

Finally the owner, exasperated, turned to him and said, "Look, boy, I don't seem to have made myself clear to you. You're not going to educate your people in this community at my expense."

As with the advocates of the poll tax, you can give this station owner credit for his lack of hypocrisy. If only we could get comparably straight talk from today's cable and broadcast network executives.

Because clearly one of the consequences of their cutting back on serious news coverage, and their substitution of sports, reality shows and other diversions – whatever may be their intentions – creates a national level of ignorance comparable to that small southern town.

You may know the story of the pollster who stopped a fellow on the street and asked him, "What's the worst problem in this community, ignorance or apathy?" The fellow stared at the pollster for a moment, and just before he walked on said, "I don't know and I don't care."

Is television programming the sole cause of ignorance and apathy in our country? Is it the sole reason why half of the potentially eligible voters don't even bother to go to the polls? Of course not. But it seems equally clear that it is one of the more significant forces at work.

Is there an "establishment" made up of a handful of wealthy individuals who have breakfast every morning and decide what they are going to try to make the American people believe that day? Not in any restaurant I go to.

But they don't have to. They already have what they need. So I will ask you to imagine the reverse. Imagine:

- What if there was some evidence that, as a result of the mindless televised distractions offered us by the television networks and cable companies, there was an ever-increasing number of progressive political activists?

- What if the percentage of non-voters was decreasing rather than increasing?

- What if the ratio between the corporate CEO's total income and his average worker's wage – once 40-to-one and now over 400-to-one – started to decline, rather than continue to increase?

- What if trade union membership began the climb back to the numbers it once enjoyed?

- What if there were more and more street demonstrations, with ever-increasing numbers, protesting corporate environmental practices and government encouragement of off-shore corporations and outsourcing jobs?

Don't you think there might be some pressure to change that televised programming? You bet there would be.

Reflect on the fact that in 2002 you were four times more likely to see a political commercial during a TV news program than an election-related news story. Do you know that the predictions are that $1.6 billion dollars will be spent on political ads in 2004?

So, you see, there's no need even to charge, let alone prove, the existence of a conspiracy. We don't need to go there. The point is that the results are the same as if there was a deliberate effort to keep the American people uninformed. The results are the same as if a network president was telling his programmers, "Look, folks, I don't seem to have made myself clear to you. You're not going to educate the people of this country at our advertisers' expense."

Manipulation Through Advertising

But as effective a political tool as ignorance may be, manipulation and misinformation are even more so.

To understand the ways in which we can be manipulated by the media's presentation of politics it is useful to remind ourselves of the manipulation to which we are subjected when the same advertising and public relations techniques are used to sell us products.

No one wants to think that they are capable of being manipulated by advertising. And yet we all are.

Take an inventory of your bathroom shelves, the brand names on your clothes, the cars you covet, the music CDs you buy (or share), even the pharmaceuticals your doctors prescribe. The odds are that a goodly number of them are among the most heavily advertised in their product line.

When I was your age or younger the question wasn't which soft drinks someone consumed, it was whether they drank that sugared syrup and water at all. Soft drinks weren't part of our daily diet. They didn't come in two-liter bottles. And they certainly didn't offer a way for school districts and universities to enrich themselves with kickbacks from monopoly suppliers of vending machines dispensing soft drinks at inflated prices. And what has made possible this substantial contribution to obesity and dental caries? Advertising.

The tobacco industry kills over 400,000 customers a year. That's more than all the deaths from alcohol, auto accidents, heroin, cocaine, fires, homicides, suicides – and the war in Iraq – combined.

Now any industry that profits from killing off its customer base soon discovers that, if it intends to stay in business, those customers need to be replaced. Since few individuals over 21 are silly enough to take up smoking, what the industry actually calls "replacement smokers" must be captured and addicted during their teen and pre-teen years – at the rate of about 3000 every day. Although these young smokers swear they can always give up smoking, if they ever try they quickly discover that nicotine is more addictive than heroin, and few succeed.

Although most of these young smokers will tell you that they are not influenced by advertising, why do you suppose that 90 percent of them smoke just three brands, the most popular being Marlboro? Would it surprise you to know that they are the three most heavily advertised brands?

In the early 20th Century cigarette smoking was something that a self-respecting young woman just wouldn't do. Since young women constituted a full half of the industry's potential but untapped market an advertising campaign was launched to reverse this thinking. Not an easy task. But today, thanks to advertising, lung cancer has become a greater threat to women's lives than breast cancer. How's that for equal rights?

Meanwhile, the power of advertising was able to convince the other half of the population – many of whom were insecure homophobic men, seeking to demonstrate their macho qualities at every opportunity – that women's cosmetics would make them sexier. By reversing these males' thinking – if anything an even more difficult undertaking than getting women to smoke – the cosmetics industry thereby widened its market by a few billion dollars.

Consumer Reports magazine has done a number of studies over the years demonstrating that it is virtually impossible for a drinker to tell the difference between brands of vodka, an alcohol known for its almost tasteless quality.

Yet consider the results of the Absolut vodka advertising campaign. When it began Absolut was selling a mere 10,000 of the 40 million cases of all brands of vodka sold that year. By campaign's end, although total industry sales had dropped to 36 million cases, Absolut's share of that market had gone from 10,000 cases to 4.5 million cases!

Think about that for a moment. Here is a product that produces $47-a-case profits, and yet is indistinguishable in taste tests from domestic brands that provide a mere $2 profit. And yet advertising is able to produce for this product a 450-fold increase in sales during a falling market.

Would you still like to argue that advertising has no impact?

Manipulation Through Political Propaganda

Let's not flatter and kid ourselves. The facts are that we can be manipulated and that we are being manipulated in order to sell us products.

So it should not be surprising that when political candidates are sold to us like toothpaste we select our favorites among them the same way we select our favorite toothpaste – on the basis of ads reflecting research with focus groups and in-depth psychological probing.

What I am about to say is not intended as criticism of our President, George W. Bush. If anything, it is praise of the extraordinary ability that he and his staff have demonstrated in maintaining his approval ratings and popular support – an essential ability, not incidentally, if any president is to be effective in serving the American people.

What I want to do is to contrast what Bush has done with what the polls show about his approval ratings. We may differ about some of the details, but grant me that what follows is ballpark correct:

- During his term he turned one of the largest federal surpluses in history to the largest deficit in history; a debt that may take decades to rectify; a debt we are leaving to our grandchildren; a debt that increases the power of the foreign nations (that are making our economy possible by buying our government's bonds) over our economic future; a debt at least in part the result of tax breaks primarily benefiting the wealthiest Americans, whom Bush described as "my base," while running up the additional costs of a major war.

- There has been less positive creation of jobs during President Bush's term than any since that of President Herbert Hoover.

- Social programs have been cut; over 40 million Americans are without health insurance; and the Administration's plan for seniors' pharmaceuticals is of primary benefit only to the big drug companies.

- Environmental protections have been cut back.

- No one argues that 9/11 was "Bush's fault." But his Administration did have intelligence that such a disaster was possible, and 9/11 did occur on his watch.

- He took a 90 percent, or more, support for America after 9/11, and turned it into a near universal opposition to our government around the world.

- Rather than continue the hunt for Osama bin Laden, originally our goal, we've turned our back on Afghanistan (where al Qaeda and the Taliban are regrouping, opium is once again the main crop, and terrorist attacks, even in Kabul, are increasing).

- We reversed decades of American foreign policy, and settled principles of international law, with the declaration that we can initiate a war in any country we choose if we think a preemptive strike is needed.

- The rationale for the Iraq war – the possession of weapons of mass destruction, a nuclear weapons program, Iraq's involvement in 9/11, the imminence of its attack on us – all proved to be, if not "lies," at least false.

- The numbers – over 1000 dead and 7000 injured Americans in 2004, not to mention 20,000 dead Iraqis, from what many see as an unnecessary war – show no signs of abating; nor does anyone (Senator Kerry, Bush, or others) seem to have a rational plan or analysis for getting us out.

As I began, the point of this enumeration is not to criticize Bush. It is to illustrate some of what he has to overcome in winning re-election. My point is that, notwithstanding these facts (or interpretations of facts), as of September 15 it looks like Bush is well on track to be re-elected.

Some of this is, of course, a result of Kerry's mistakes. The fact remains that it represents an awesome accomplishment on Bush's part.

Look at the latest polls. Bush leads, among those most likely to vote, by 52 to 43 percent over Kerry. The same percentage, 52 percent, "approve" of the great job he has been doing. (Kerry's "favorable" rating, meanwhile, has fallen from 51 to 36 percent.) Voters asked about the candidates' personal attributes give Bush the nod on honesty, leadership, vision, values and personality. The two candidates are tied for their understanding of the problems of "people like you."

Are voters for their candidate, or merely opposed to the alternative? Eighty percent of Bush's supporters are voting for Bush; only 40 percent of Kerry's supporters are for Kerry; 55 percent are simply against Bush.

These numbers are, it seems to me, the result of a stunning and remarkable accomplishment on the part of a very professionally skilled Bush team – especially given the record I have just outlined which they had to overcome.

Most significantly, the number of voters who selected "terrorism" as their top voting issue has gone from 19 percent to 25. Those who select the "economy" and "jobs" dropped from 31 percent to 25.

Why is that "most significant"? Because, as someone has observed, "even if the media does not tell us what to think, it does tell us what to think about." And when American voters are thinking about terrorism, war, national security, defense and foreign affairs, they think the Republicans are better able to deal with those issues. When they are thinking about jobs, income security, health care, and social welfare they think the Democrats' candidate is the better choice.

That's not to say these perceptions of voters are accurate. But, then, it doesn't matter if they're accurate or not. As long as they are what voters believe, campaigns need to take them into account.

In other words, it matters not so much what you communicate about your candidate as it does what subjects you get the media, and the electorate, to think and talk about.

From this perspective, Kerry's focus on what have historically been "Republican issues" may turn out to be a fundamental strategic error of monumental proportions and the cause of his losing the election.

For it should have come as no surprise to the Kerry camp that, as the polls report, "Bush holds significant advantages over Kerry on who would be best equipped to deal with terrorism, Iraq and . . . relations with other countries." Notwithstanding the results in Iraq, and the increase in numbers of anti-American terrorists and terrorist attacks, only 45 percent think the war was not worth fighting, and 52 percent think the U.S. government can prevent terrorist attacks on our country.

It is difficult for a writer or speaker to draw lessons from Nazi Germany. When one does, the response is so often the outrage of a reader or listener who jumps to the conclusion that the author or speaker is charging some American with being, in every particular, "just like Hitler."

This is so silly. No one thinks that because Hitler built the autobahns ("interstate highway system") in Germany, and President Dwight Eisenhower built the interstate highway system in the U.S., that Eisenhower (who defeated Hitler) is "just like Hitler."

So let's see what we can learn from Nazi propaganda without going crazy thinking that I am charging Kerry, Bush, Clinton, Gore or some other politician with being a Hitler. The fact is that many of the techniques of advertising and public relations that were developed in the early 20th Century knew then, and know now, no national boundaries.

Unlike "Fahrenheit 911," one of the advantages of using the movie "Wag the Dog" for examples is that it is essentially bi-partisan. You've probably seen the film. If not, the president in the film is confronting a scandal over a sexual encounter with a young girl in the oval office. (Sound familiar?) The public relations response, to divert the media's attention from the bad news weeks before an election, is to start a war. (Also familiar.)

Many nations' leaders have looked for diversionary news when things aren't going well, and wars have been one of their more popular choices.

Can you identify the source of the following comments on the subject?

"Naturally the common people don't want war; neither in Russia, nor in England, nor in America, nor in Germany. That is understood. But after all, it is the leaders of the country who determine policy, and it is always a simple matter to drag the people along, whether it is a democracy, or a fascist dictatorship, or a parliament, or a communist dictatorship. Voice or no voice, the people can always be brought to the bidding of the leaders. That is easy. All you have to do is to tell them they are being attacked, and denounce the pacifists for lack of patriotism and exposing the country to danger. It works the same in any country."

The author? Nazi Germany's Hermann Goering in 1946.

The online *Washington Post* carried a report of Vice President Cheney's comments during campaign appearances September 7, 2004.

You tell me, is Cheney charging that Kerry is, to use Goering's words, "exposing the country to danger"? Here's what he said:

"It's absolutely essential that eight weeks from today, on November 2nd, we make the right choice, because if we make the wrong choice then the danger is that we'll get hit again . . . in a way that will be devastating from the standpoint of the United States . . .." (emphasis supplied)

Ironically, in the online version the story was positioned under a Burger King ad with the line, "Enjoy an original Whopper today."

Whopper or not, subsequent apologies about how that's not really what he meant or not, statements like Cheney's – as Goering noted – do have their political effect.

Moreover, they have a lasting effect.

Cheney can apologize. He can say he didn't really mean it that way. We can learn other things about the terrorist threat in general, and Kerry in particular, that override the suggestion. But it remains with us, at least unconsciously, and will accompany us into the voting booth next November.

As I began, Cheney's use of this Goering line doesn't transform "Wag the Dog" from entertaining fiction to enlightening fact. It does not challenge the wisdom (or not) of our going to war with Iraq. It doesn't mean that the Kerry camp's tactics and rhetoric are any better than those of the Bush folks. And it certainly does not suggest that Cheney is Goering or that President Bush has anything in common with Hitler.

But when we ask, "What's a voter to do?" one answer is that voters might want to become much more skeptical and questioning about what their government is telling them – regardless of what country they live in and which party happens to be in power at the moment.

Consider the observation of Hitler's Minister of Propaganda, Joseph Goebbels. He said: "If you tell a lie big enough and keep repeating it, people will eventually come to believe it." Could that still be true in this country, today, with our superior educational system and our access to a wide range of media outlets?

Consider the results reported last year by the University of Maryland's Program on International Policy Attitudes entitled "Misperceptions, the Media and the Iraq War," October 2, 2003.

In the course of three polls last year, over 3300 persons, all of whom follow the news fairly closely, were asked which broadcast or print sources provide most of their news. They were then asked questions regarding three propositions:

1. There was "clear evidence in Iraq that Saddam Hussein was working closely with the al Qaeda terrorist organization."

2. "The U.S. has found Iraqi weapons of mass destruction."

3. "The majority of people [in the world] favor the U.S. having gone to war."

Each of these propositions is false. You may want to quibble with me about the details. But most people would not, and even those who do would concede, I hope, that the statements are mostly false.

What the polling revealed, however, is that – even after correcting for demographic differences – 80 percent of those who primarily rely on Fox as the source of their news had a misperception about one or more of these propositions. By contrast, only 47 percent of those who primarily rely on print sources had such misperceptions, and a mere 23 percent of those whose primary source is NPR got any wrong answers.

The Fox-NPR split on false perceptions about Hussein's ties to al Qaeda was 67 percent to 16 percent. For WMD it was 33 percent to 11 percent, and for world opinion 35 percent to 5 percent.

For most television and news outlets it didn't make much difference – in terms of the viewers' misperceptions – how closely they were paying attention. The only exception was Fox. The most responsible Fox viewers, those who paid really close attention, ended up with more misperceptions than those who were more casual about following Fox's take on the news.

Moreover, these misperceptions translate into support for the president. Those who indicated they would vote for the president held misperceptions 45 percent of the time; those who would not vote for the president only held misperceptions 17 percent of the time.

Clearly, what we watch, what we are told by the media, does influence our political positions on the issues and choices from among candidates.

We needn't, like Joseph Goebbels, speak of "lies." Let's just say "if you can get the media to televise a misperception big enough, and get them to repeat it often enough, people will eventually come to believe it."

What a Voter Can Do

So "what's a voter to do?"

Many of the things you can do don't necessarily involve the media. And you know them already.

You can make sure you're registered to vote – and register others. You can help get absentee ballots to those who want them – and use one yourself. You can make it a habit to vote in all elections – party primaries, school board and city council elections – not just the presidential and other general elections every four years. And you can take family members and friends with you.

When the time comes that you have children of your own, take them with you to the polls. That will do as much to insure their active political participation in later years as anything you could do.

You can select a party and become active. Maybe two; a party for your heart, like the Greens or Libertarians, and one of the two major parties for your head.

Recall what the 19th Century New York City political Boss William Tweed is credited with having said, "I don't care who does the electing just so long as I do the nominating."

Don't let Boss Tweed's descendents continue to do all the nominating, leaving you with nothing but the electing.

After you've had some experience working in others' campaigns, consider running for office yourself.

What Voters Can Do With the Internet

We've touched on some of the problems with television, radio and the newspapers.

Fortunately for all of us, there's a whole new medium of individual and mass communication out there: the Internet.

If you are not already aware of them, there are two outstanding sites to help you get accurate information about the candidates.

One is Project Vote Smart at http://www.vote-smart.org. At its site you can look up any race, in any state, and find out virtually anything you'd want to know about a candidate, including his or her positions on the issues. It provides you links to biographical information, candidates' campaign finances, how they've been rated by interest groups, their public statements and, if they are already in office, their voting records.

Candidates don't like to discuss the real issues, or reveal their positions. So how does Project Vote Smart find out? It administers the "National Political Awareness Test" to each of them – or, more accurately, each candidate who responds.

Have your senators and members of congress responded? If not

- You might want to call their offices in Washington, or their campaign headquarters, and ask what they're afraid of.

- You might want to talk to your newspapers' publishers and editors, and broadcast news directors, and tell them you'd like their help in getting these candidates' cooperation.

- Or write letters to the editor, and call in to talk shows, to ask why your officials haven't responded.

Because of the major role of money in campaigns, the resulting corruption of our legislative process, and the major parties' belief that public disclosure is the only protection we need, we have an obligation to find out which special interests have purchased our representatives.

One of the places you can do this online is the Center for Responsive Politics' Web site, Open Secrets, http://www.opensecrets.org. It offers you about as many ways to slice this information as you could ever want or even imagine. Present records and past records. Contributions and financial disclosure forms. Contributors by name and by industry group. Searches on names or zip codes. Who has given, who has received, and how much.

If you want to do a little more research on your own you can try to figure out the relationships between what the contributors pay and what they get.

For example, did you ever wonder why, with all the popular pressure for control of escalating pharmaceutical prices, the Congress did nothing effective to control them? No price controls. No direct government purchasing. Congress forbids our importing medicines from Canada at a fraction of the U.S. price. Congress won't even discuss the way the government uses our tax money to develop new pharmaceutical products that are then handed over to pharmaceutical companies, rather than being made available to all as generics.

Seems odd, doesn't it? Does it help you to understand to know that during the 2002 election cycle the pharmaceutical industry gave members of Congress $30 million dollars in what they persist in calling "campaign contributions" rather than "bribes"?

What did they get? Between 1995 and 2001 the money spent on prescription drugs went from $64 to $154 billion.

The federal Center for Medicare & Medicaid Services projects total health care costs of $3.1 trillion a year by 2012 and you can bet, with the help of their friends in Congress, the pharmaceutical industry will continue to get more than their fair share of that increase as well.

There are a lot of governmental decisions that become much more understandable once you "follow the money." I did a study some years ago to see if there was some direct relationship between campaign contributions and corporate profits. It turns out there is. I won't walk you through all the examples and analysis, but the bottom line is that the usual return on these "investments" is 1000-to-2000 to one. A $10,000 contribution produces $10 million; $1 million in soft money contributions will produce between $1 and $2 billion in benefits from a grateful government.

Media Reform

During the 1970s I was chair of a media reform organization called the National Citizens Committee for Broadcasting. I soon found it was much easier to accomplish our mission as a part of a coalition, rather than going it alone.

In the course of building those coalitions, I would say to other public interest groups, "Whatever is your first priority, whether it is women's rights or saving wildlife, your second priority has to be media reform. With it you at least have a chance of accomplishing your first priority. Without it, you don't have a prayer."

Once you have studied the issues you will come up with your own list of media reform priorities. But I suspect it will include a focus on greater diversity in media ownership, permitting more participation in the presidential debates, some amount of free radio and TV time for all candidates, public financing of campaigns, a re-enactment of the Fairness Doctrine and the personal attack rules, an FCC requirement of public service announcements, and a gradual working toward a goal of separating content from conduit.

If this is something that interests you, there are a number of organizations you can contact that have already done much of the groundwork for you. You may just want to read what they've put up on the Web. Or you may actually want to contribute money, become a member, apply for an internship, or go to work for them.

So "what's a voter to do"?

Learn the things you will learn if you are paying attention to the ways in which the politicians and media are trying to manipulate you.

And then read the books, and the Web sites, and do what they say.

INDEX